iChange
Invest in Changing Yourself

Alan Lyons

MANAGEMENT BRIEFS

Essential Insights for Busy Managers

All design, artwork and liaison with printers has been undertaken by
Graphics 4U, 6 Coill Beag, Ratoath, Co. Meath.
Image concepts: Aisli Madden of Design BOS.
Portrait photograph: Phillip Martin Photography.

Publisher: **Management Briefs,** 30 The Palms, Clonskeagh, Dublin 14.

Table of Contents

To the wellbeing of my wife Bex and
our children, Ivy and Hugo.

Alan Lyons
November 2013

Introduction

> *"No problem can be solved by the same*
> *level of consciousness that created it."*
>
> *Albert Einstein*

This book is intended to provide you with an overview of a compelling approach to personal change.

Chapter 1 explores the varying approaches people take to change and the impact that these approaches can have. Chapter 2 contrasts the habit of predominantly cultivating 'a problem view' over 'a solution view' and the business case for developing the latter.

Chapters 3 to 7 outline a step-by-step approach to implementing a compelling model for change - the solution turbine. The model enhances mental toughness and resilience which is especially useful when dealing with unpredictability and/or adversity. Each stage of the solution turbine provides a sequential approach to the next stage, allowing you to progressively journey towards your optimal functioning state which will see you free to make an authentic contribution.

Chapter 8 looks at the usefulness of the solution turbine in various applications within organisations and teams.

Finally, chapter 9 outlines a brief synopsis of how I got here.

Enjoy being inside iChange!

Alan Lyons

November 2013

1

Change the Viewing
to Change the Doing

Chapter outline

→ The Power of Expectations on What
   we View
→ Multiple Intelligences
→ Our Brains are Plastic
→ Change is Inevitable
→ Growth Mindset
→ Real Change: Put on your own Oxygen
   Mask First!
→ Re-evaluating Resistance

> "No person is like this or like that. People change all the time. "

> *Tom Andersen*

Differing Viewpoints

In George Bernard Shaw's Pygmalion, Eliza Doolittle explains:

'You see, really and truly, apart from the things anyone can pick up (the dressing and the proper way of speaking, and so on), the difference between a lady and a flower girl is not how she behaves but how she's treated. I shall always be a flower girl to Professor Higgins because he always treats me as a flower girl and always will; but I know I can be a lady to you because you always treat me as a lady and always will.'

Eliza Doolittle illustrates a concept known as a self-fulfilling prophecy. A self-fulfilling prophecy takes place when we have certain expectations or aspirations. We communicate them in many ways often unknowingly, and without always intending to. Those we interact with often adjust their thinking and behaviours as a consequence of the signals we give out and this creates a self-fulfilling prophecy.

We can all remember someone who ignited our potential, maybe a sport's coach, a teacher or someone who held a position of influence. This person is likely to have had a greater impact on your success in life than your IQ, schooling or family background because they had high expectations for you. Unfortunately the opposite is also true. If a teacher expects nothing of a student, even when s/he is trying to hide their low expectation, it is often communicated unintentionally. When this is consciously or unconsciously communicated to the student they perform according to the low expectation, making it a self-fulfilling prophecy.

Psychologists Rosenthal and Jacobson carried out research into the power of expectations named the Pygmalion Effect after Shaw's play. In their study, teachers at a school were given fabricated IQ results of the students in their classes. The teachers were further led to believe that the results also tested for academic potential. Interestingly, the students whom the teachers were told would most likely perform better academically did so. The teachers also reported that those particular students were more courteous, friendly, curious and better behaved when compared to their counterparts. The teachers quite clearly saw what they expected to see.

However, the really amazing part is that the students picked up on the expectations clues, many unconscious, given by the teachers and responded accordingly.

The power of expectations and self-fulfilling prophecies clearly demonstrates that the way we view a situation will have an impact on what we do and the outcomes we achieve.

Multiple Intelligences

Research indicates that the best predictor of success in life often has little to do with a person's IQ. Were such findings and the idea of multiple intelligences ever made available to you while at school or during your career? I imagine not. Essentially people are not equally 'smart' or 'dumb' under all circumstances, rather it's to do with which intelligences they seek to nourish or disregard. The particular intelligences we enhance depend on what we value and deem important to us. This also underplays the maxim of 'use it or loose it'.

Our Brains are plastic

As they say in the L'Oreal advertisement "Here comes the science bit..." Recent neuro-scientific research shows us that our brains are in part 'plastic' and contrary to popular opinion, we are not 'either/or' by nature. Our brains are changeable - luckily. We can activate and develop new neural pathways in our brains which enable us to function better at a solution focused and emotional level. Emotions respond just like muscles in that the ones you stimulate the most become the strongest and most accessible when you need them most. Whilst you may currently have a dusty back road infrastructure operating your brain, you can develop new neurons, connections and build a solution focused, super lane multi-highway!

Change is Inevitable

"You cannot step into the same river twice."

Heraclites

We are not the same people today as we were yesterday. Change is occurring all the time and nothing remains at the same level of intensity. Even being aware of this can increase your resilience levels. If we believe we can't succeed or ever change, this feeling of being stuck can lead to a dependent psychological condition called 'learned helplessness'. This occurs when people act helpless, even when they have the power to change.

5

Growth Mindset

"If you're not making mistakes, then you're not doing anything. I'm positive that a doer makes mistakes."
John Wooden

Carol Dweck wrote the book Mindset: The New Psychology of Success. Its central message is that if you have a fixed mindset then you believe the abilities and talents you currently possess are pretty much it. This way of thinking means you believe that changes to your general intelligence levels are extremely limited. In contrast growth mindset people believe that their abilities and talents are continually developing and that they have the capacity to change and grow. Unsurprisingly Dweck explains how a growth mindset is essential for success.

People often talk about natural talent as if it is the 'holy grail' and the only way anyone great every achieved something i.e. little effort but massive 'natural ability'. However, once you scratch beneath the surface of these so called natural talents you nearly always find quite a different picture and one that normally involves a lot of hard grit, sweat, determination and practice. For instance, the American basketball player Michael Jordan, considered one of the most naturally talented players of all time, practised hoops on the court after training and matches long after his team mates had gone home. Einstein did not pass his final school exams...the list goes on and on.

The message is that behind the appearance of natural talent or extreme intelligence there is quite often a lot of hard work and practice. In fact people who are labelled talented or highly intelligent at a young age often underperform and fail to live up to their early expectations. Early identification of supposedly innate talents often sees the individual put in limited effort as they expect it all to naturally happen for them. This is why the people who start out the smartest in life do not necessarily end up the smartest. This is also why fixed mindset people are often very defensive to any feedback. Their inner belief that they do not have the capacity to change means that feedback is perceived as a direct attack on their self-esteem. In contrast a growth mindset individual seeks out feedback because they view it as useful material to help them to flourish and develop.

Read the following four sentences and write down whether you agree or disagree with each of them:

1. **You are a certain kind of person, and there is not much that can be done to really change that.**

2. **No matter what kind of person you are, you can always change substantially.**

3. **You can do things differently, but the important parts of who you are can't really be changed.**

4. **You can always change basic things about the kind of person you are.**

Answering yes to 1 and 3 reflects someone with a 'fixed mindset' and yes to 2 and 4 reflects someone who would tend to have to a 'growth mindset'.

Which answers do you agree more with? Solution focused individuals utilise a growth mindset stretching themselves, taking risks, accepting feedback, and taking a long-term view by focusing on possibilities.

Real Change: Put on your own Oxygen mask first!

"I'm starting with the man in the mirror."

Michael Jackson

Why does an airplane pilot tell us to put on our own oxygen mask first in the event of a sudden loss in cabin pressure? This is because we should not seek to help others until we have first worked on ourselves. Essentially we have to work towards our own flourishing in advance of looking at optimal ways of interacting with others.

Many people believe their lives will be better once 'this' person or 'that' person changes their behaviour towards them. However, trying to change others who do not want to change is often impossible and a terrible waste of time and emotional energy. Thankfully, there is a useful alternative and that is that you can change yourself and in doing so quite often change the way in which people behave towards you.

"They cannot take away our self-respect if we do not give it to them."

Mahatma Ghandi

Many clients I see have a sense that their happiness is dependent on others changing first or making the first move. This gives complete control over to others. Often victims of bullying are energised when they realise that changing the way in which they choose to respond can also change others' behaviour towards them. We will be addressing how to make such solution focused strategies work in your own particular circumstance. Essentially building on Ghandi's teaching, the only power people have over you is the power you give them. The trick is to not let how we feel or act to be dictated by other people's emotional weaknesses and/or failings in their actions towards us.

Re-evaluating Resistance

Lastly, contrary to popular opinion, people are not generally resistant to change. However, they quite often do not respond well to forced change or change that they do not feel meaningfully involved in. Resistance is no longer considered a useful concept by many. Interestingly psychoanalyst Sigmund Freud used the term 'resistance' as a form of name calling when a client did not champion one of the expert-led and problem focused ideas he came up with for them. In contrast a solution view accepts clients as the experts on themselves.

The solution focus approach seeks to push the door with a client and not against them. Remember that you can't change anyone else without their permission or unless it makes sense to them. They may appear accepting but they could really be derailing your efforts so as to protect themselves (from what you want for them). As with a coaching client who has being instructed to consult with me, it is usually a waste of their time unless they want to be there.

Summary of Chapter 1

How we view a situation greatly impacts what we do and the outcomes we achieve.

→ If you want to make a small difference you can adapt certain behaviours however if you want to make a big splash work on your mindset.

→ Science shows us that we will benefit from looking at our intelligences differently.

→ Change is a constant in everyone's life.

→ Certain beliefs you hold about your mind's capacity for growth can influence dramatically your ability to realise your full potential.

→ People often try to change others before themselves which is often less successful.

→ The illusion of resistance appears if individuals do not feel meaningfully involved in what is taking place.

2 A Solution View

Chapter outline

→ Differing Viewpoints
→ View-Do-Outcome
→ The Habit of Pessimism
→ Smart Optimism
→ Smart Optimism v. Blind Optimism
→ Luck is not a Factor
→ The Knowledge-Age Worker Connection
→ Cultivating Positive Emotion

"Men are disturbed not by things, but by the view which they take of them.

Epictetus, Ancient Greek Philosopher

Differing Viewpoints

We all construct our own view of the way in which we see the world. This is our reality. Our standpoint or view can have a big impact on the results we get and influence greatly how likely we are to be operating at our optimal level. There are numerous factors that influence our view of our environment, many of which are reliant on the culture in which we are immersed. These factors include our friends, family and our work. This creates our view of the world - our 'mental map'.

View - Do - Outcome

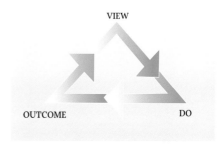

The cyclical diagram above illustrates the way in which our view influences our actions and therefore the outcomes that we get from those actions. With this in mind the two diagrams below demonstrate the difference between taking a problem view or a solution view and illustrate how the view that we take effects the outcome and results we achieve.

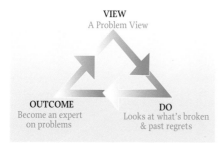

When your view is in line with what works best for you, it is more likely that you will be operating at your optimal level and experiencing enhanced outcomes.

"Whether you believe you can do a thing or not, you are right."

Henry Ford

Before Roger Bannister ran a mile in less than four minutes in 1954 it was looked at with a problem view and deemed impossible. In fact medical doctors (who are experts on problems!) stated in various medical journals of the day that the human body could not withstand such an achievement as the pressure would cause the heart to combust. Unsurprisingly most athletes believed it impossible (problem view) so they trained without it as a goal (do) and their best achievements were confined to the experts' view of the implausibility of running a sub four minute mile (outcome). Bannister instead took a solution view by breaking the mile down into doable chunks by focusing on the distance he needed to run every 30 seconds in order to accomplish a sub four minute mile. Interestingly within 18 months of Bannister smashing the myth, 39 other athletes also ran a sub four minute mile. Bear in mind that these athletes did

not take performance enhancing drugs or use a new enlightened training regime, they simply viewed running a sub four minute mile differently. As Carl Rogers would say they changed the viewing to change the doing. This story illustrates the extraordinary positive impact a solution view can make.

A problem view can of course be effective at times. Particularly in jobs where there is an obvious 'cause and effect' to solving a problem such as with mechanics. However what works well when looking under the bonnet of car does not work so well with people.

An optimistic mindset is at the heart of being solution focused. People often claim that they are not pessimistic but that they are 'realistic'. This is normally followed by the statement 'that is why there is no point trying'. However, being realistic means you should be open to possibilities and exploring differences, which by its very nature is being optimistic as 'realistic-ally' a solution might exist! A pessimistic person is the same as a problem focused person. They inhibit creativity and lateral thinking. Think of a team meeting where even before it commences someone lists all the reasons why something won't work - all positive energy is sapped from the room and a feeling of inertia quickly sets in.

However, the opposite is equally true. Take a moment to think of a successful person you enjoy the company of and admire. Are they pessimistic or optimistic by nature? It is likely that they are optimistic as research shows that this attribute is highly predictive of someone's success in life. It is also a contagious attribute which magnetically draws people to them. More often people enjoy and admire optimistic people as they start from the premise of exploring what might be, as opposed to a definitive 'can't' or 'shan't'.

The Habit of Pessimism

Evolution plays a significant part. Being problem focused and reactive is what enabled our ancestor, the caveman, to survive. People often think that by fully understanding a problem they will arrive at a solution or that understanding failure will mean they are more likely to achieve success. Whilst this might happen, it is more likely to waste a huge amount of your energy, time and resources. This thinking often leads to a 'paralysis by analysis' situation.

Being problem focused or pessimistic is a habit which is a learned mindset. It is also easier to be a critic or a naysayer. By breaking such a pattern you can learn to be more solution focused.

"Habits of thinking need not be forever...individuals can choose the way they think."

Martin Seligman

Smart Optimism

The most successful solution focused people utilise what I call 'smart optimism'. As mentioned, people make sense of their lives by how they view, experience or interpret particular events, which is generally either optimistically or pessimistically (i.e. utilising a problem focus or a solution focus). Psychologists call this idea 'attribution theory'. Martin Seligman, acclaimed psychologist and author of Learned Optimism lists three ways in which the thinking of optimistic people differs from that of pessimistic people. The optimistic thinker believes their experiences to be mostly local, changeable and temporary. Interestingly these are the ways in which solution focused people build resilience through how they interpret setbacks as outlined below.

Optimistic Attribution Style: The Solution Focus View

1. Local: **It is only a snapshot in time and it is only one situation**

2. Changeable: **I can influence certain things and change is a constant**

3. Temporary: **Nothing lasts forever and I have coped before**

Interestingly Seligman could frequently predict who would win the U.S. National Basketball Association (NBA) finals by viewing transcripts of post-match interviews made by athletes and their coaches to the media prior to the final. He predicted (correctly) that the teams where the majority of the players used a solution focused view and language after winning, or being beaten, were more likely to win in the final. Essentially optimistic players saw failures as more temporary, changeable and locally caused. A pessimist however tends to view a set-back as more permanent, universal (wide in scope) and internal, thereby believing that it reflects a fundamental weakness or personal failing which is very difficult to do anything about. Seligman continually found that if you have two teams of broadly equal abilities but one team is more optimistic, and the other team is more pessimistic, then the more optimistic team will recover better from setbacks.

"The pessimist sees the difficulty in every opportunity; the optimist sees the opportunity in every difficulty. "

Winston Churchill

Sir Winston Churchill fought depression and had a long rocky road to navigate before becoming Prime Minister of the UK in 1940. He often referred to his depression as 'the black dog' being upon him. By describing his depression in these terms he embraced a solution view, even the terminology suggests temporality and separation between him and the condition. Granted it did not cure or completely relieve him of his severe depression. It did however enable him to cope with it more effectively which allowed him to make a significant authentic contribution during his lifetime.

Solution focused people take control by focusing on everything they can influence and that which may assist them in getting a better result. They are not reactive or problem-focused individuals who blame everything on their environment, their boss or a terrible childhood. Rather they make choices that allow them to focus on things that are controllable and predictable about their future. This is the engine room and is at the heart of the solution turbine model that we will explore in the next chapter.

Smart Optimism v. Blind Optimism

As mentioned, the solution focus uses what I call 'smart optimism'. The diagram below illustrates the difference between smart optimism and blind optimism.

Unfortunately positive psychology can sometimes be confused with relentless positivity, which I refer to as 'blind optimism'.

	LOW ANALYSIS	HIGH ANALYSIS
High Trust	BLIND OPTIMISM	
Low Trust		SMART OPTIMISM

Smart optimism involves rigorous thought and analysis. In this way decisions are reached when all possibilities have been explored. This is particularly important when there are low levels of trust involved. While smart optimism is curious and hopeful as a way of responding to a situation it is not redundant if the outcome or result is not the initially desired one. A person may want to play for the New Zealand rugby team as a forward. However if you are small in stature it is likely to be a goal that leads to disappointment. Smart optimism in such a scenario may make you willing to improve while analysing more preferable positions or indeed sports. In Jim Collins's book *Good to Great* he outlines a perfect example of smart optimism in what he refers to as the 'Stockdale Paradox'. Jim Stockdale was a U.S. prisoner of war in Vietnam who suffered severe torture over a period of seven years. He noted that the soldiers who thought that they would be released by Christmas ('blind optimism') were less likely to survive and more likely to commit suicide in the horrendous circumstances rather than the ones who embraced 'smart optimism'. Stockdale explained the 'Stockdale Paradox' by stating, "You must never confuse faith that you will prevail in the end - which you can never afford to lose - with the discipline to confront the most brutal facts of your current reality, whatever that might be."

Luck is Not a Factor

Choosing to be solution focused expands your potential and allows you to tap into your underutilised and potentially dormant resources. This enables you to function at your optimal level which is good for your mind, heart, body and spirit. Solution focused people are often thought of as lucky individuals, especially by more problem focused people. In his book called The Luck Factor, psychologist Richard Wiseman refutes the myth that some people are born lucky. He explores the principles that lead people to consider themselves 'lucky'. These I believe are all solution focused mindsets and behaviours which are summarised below.

Richard Wiseman's Luck Factor Principles:

→ Principle One: Maximise your Chance Opportunities

   Solution Focus: Be open to new experiences and bounce back from setbacks

→ Principle Two: Listen to your Lucky Hunches

   Solution Focus: Visualise what you want to achieve and set goals to make it happen

→ Principle Three: Expect Good Fortune

   Solution Focus: Continual positive expectation acts as a self-fulfilling prophecy

→ Principle Four: Turn your Bad Luck into Good

   Solution Focus: Focus on and amplify what is working even when things are not going to plan and pull strengths from them

Journalist Paul B. Carroll describes a solution focused conversation that took place in the 1960s when an IBM executive made a decision that ended up losing IBM $10 million, the equivalent of €70 million today. Carroll described what happened next:

As the executive cowered, Watson asked, 'Do you know why I've asked you here?'

The man replied, 'I assume I'm here so you can fire me.'

Watson looked surprised.

'Fire you?' he asked. 'Of course not. I just spent $10 million educating you.'

A solution view and the cultivation of optimism all lead to the development of mental toughness and independence of mind. It makes you less self-doubting and more trusting of yourself. Rudyard Kipling's poem 'If' elegantly captures the essence of a solution view.

If

If you can keep your head when all about you
Are losing theirs and blaming it on you;
If you can trust yourself when all men doubt you,
But make allowance for their doubting too;
If you can wait and not be tired by waiting,
Or, being lied about, don't deal in lies,
Or, being hated, don't give way to hating,
And yet don't look too good, nor talk too wise;

If you can dream - and not make dreams your master;
If you can think - and not make thoughts your aim;
If you can meet with triumph and disaster
And treat those two imposters just the same;
If you can bear to hear the truth you've spoken
Twisted by knaves to make a trap for fools,
Or watch the things you gave your life to broken,
And stoop and build 'em up with wornout tools;

If you can make one heap of all your winnings
And risk it on one turn of pitch-and-toss,
And lose, and start again at your beginnings
And never breath a word about your loss;
If you can force your heart and nerve and sinew
To serve your turn long after they are gone,
And so hold on when there is nothing in you
Except the Will which says to them: 'Hold on';

If you can talk with crowds and keep your virtue,
Or walk with kings - nor lose the common touch;
If neither foes nor loving friends can hurt you;
If all men count with you, but none too much;
If you can fill the unforgiving minute
With sixty seconds' worth of distance run -
Yours is the Earth and everything that's in it,
And - which is more - you'll be a Man my son!

Rudyard Kipling

The Knowledge-Age Worker Connection

My work brings me into contact with a diverse range of professionals from physicists to financiers. These individuals often manage people like machines with a fixed mindset belonging to the industrial age. Such an approach in the time of knowledge-age work is timely, costly and ultimately ineffective. An industrial age worker's most useful piece of technology was their manual tools whilst a knowledge-age worker's most useful piece of technology is their minds. Today's workers are required to manage their own decision-making, energy and attention. Knowledge-age workers are best led through the heart, body, mind and spirit. A solution focus enables just this. Understanding how to manage the emotions behind actions is the difference that can make a positive one - by engaging people's 'being'.

> "The most important, and indeed the truly unique contribution of management in the 20th century was the fifty - fold increase in the productivity of the manual worker. The most important contribution management needs to make in the 21st century is similarly to increase the productivity of knowledge work and the knowledge worker."
>
> *Peter Drucker, Father of Modern Management*

Cultivating Positive Emotion

Employers often consider loyalty, engagement and performance as the qualities that matter most in an employee. Research by psychologists such as Barbara Fredickson, shows that these qualities are best achieved by creating positive emotion. Whilst a manager who employs bullying techniques might get an immediate result through fear, this management style will not be building a future or enhance the employee's or manager's engagement or resilience levels.

Fredickson refers to building on positive emotions and potential for the future through her 'broaden and build' theory of positive emotion. She explains that broadening the repertoire of a person's creative responses leads to an increase in their personal resources. Through this flow of positive emotion we learn new ways of 'viewing to change the doing'; whilst also becoming more resilient to setbacks. At a team level the 'broaden and build' theory operates very well when leaders blend the appropriate level of support with challenge. If the team perceives the creation of positive emotion to have been set about with integrity, as in a leader who is visibly authentic and credible, it can foster creativity and resourcefulness.

The right balance between a supportive and challenging environment unleashes the creative potential of the whole team. This enhanced level of competence and resources has the ability to increase productivity, profitability as well as customer and employee loyalty.

Positive emotions broaden our thought-action repertoires - such as the feeling of joy which makes us want to play, a sense of interest and intrigue that makes us want to explore. Positive emotions allow people to tap into their physical, social, intellectual and psychological resources and thereby take care of their whole-being.

The opposite is also true, with negative emotion, our thought-action repertoire is one of fear where we just want the ground to open up and swallow us up. I remember sitting on an interview panel when an apparently pleasant fellow interviewer turned into a Gestapo type character when the interviewee arrived. Somehow he understood that his job was to scare the candidates by injecting them with negative emotion. This left us observing the candidates at their worst. Why? Surely we wanted to see them at their best. Whilst this technique might have its place in C.I.A. interviews it seems paradoxical in less potentially interrogatory roles. Positive emotions allow us to perform as well in front of others as we could when we know no one is watching. Again it allows us to be ourselves with more skill.

The surge of a synergy that is created by positive emotion between an individual and their sense of meaningful involvement within an organisation will at the same time increase personal well-being and therefore improve an organisation's outcomes. And remember a culture is created by what most people are doing most of the time.

Research clearly shows how simple acts of honest appreciation can encourage people, whether they are recovering from a stroke, to a boss appreciating the contribution an employee is endeavoring to make. Declan Kidney, the most successful manager of an Irish rugby team in the professional era, leverages his understanding of the power of positive emotions by placing good luck messages from supporters, friends and family in the changing rooms for the players to view as they are getting psyched up before a big game.

As mentioned if you are in the flow of positive emotions you are more likely to be creative, confident and to diminish the way you view a setback. Negative stimulation will not become overwhelming and you will cope well and become more and more resilient over time. There is also much research to support the hypothesis that enduring positive emotion can prevent depression, protect against heart disease and triggers an upward spiral to increase wellbeing as well as building optimism, tranquillity, and resilience. Fredrickson's research indicates that a positive ratio of 3:1 (i.e. where a person experiences 3 positives to every negative emotion) is the base level at which you can start to flourish and reap the benefits of positive emotion. A 5:1 ratio indicates you are flourishing. The solution turbine process you are about to explore is an excellent way to enhance your positivity ratio. As an aside, if you're a fan of the British television soap EastEnders you might be interested to know that each episode contains on average a negative ratio of 11:1, just think of the psychological malnourishment being experienced prior to going to bed for a supposed restful night's sleep! The Simpsons cartoon contains the highest positivity ratio of any show measured which will leave you with a refreshing sense of wellbeing - if you enjoy the cartoon that is!

Summary of Chapter 2

→ A solution view unleashes the power of positive psychology into your life.

→ Problem focused individuals cultivate a habit of pessimism.

→ Optimistic individuals effectively view setbacks as local, changeable and temporary.

→ With a solution view we pay greater attention to what matters most and make better choices.

→ A problem view belongs to the age of control and command management and a solution view to the new era of the knowledge-age worker.

→ An awareness of how we think, react and understand our environment improves personal effectiveness, fulfillment and our decision making capability.

→ The creation of positive emotion is essential for people to feel they can flourish and perform more consistently at their ideal performance state.

→ Research indicates that a positivity ratio of 3:1 is the base level at which we can start to flourish. Strive for 5:1!

3 Be Solution Focused

Chapter outline

→ The Solution Turbine Model
→ Useful Conversations
→ Frame of Reference
→ Solution Focused Questioning
→ Solution Focused Language Tips
→ Respond v. React
→ Event - Solution Choice - Respond
→ Control the Controllables
→ The Solution Focus Tool

The Solution Turbine Model

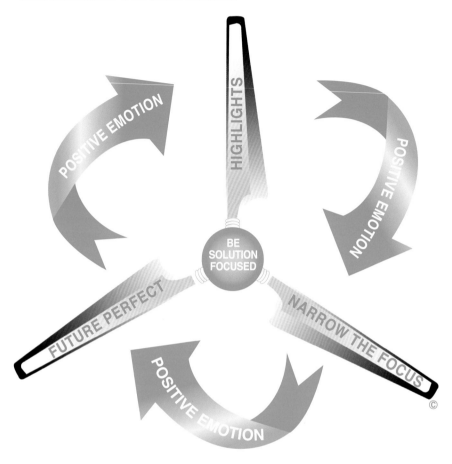

The solution turbine embraces a radically new paradigm for taking a positive approach to change. It contains four elements that incorporate what is predictable and controllable about engaging with change. It simplifies and does not seek to over-complicate the experience of change. The turbine is propelled by the positive emotions that drive high performance. It applies the science behind positive psychology and high performance to enable people to focus their time, attention and energy on making an authentic contribution.

The 4 Components of the *Solution Turbine*

Your Authentic Contribution

A clearly defined authentic contribution instils meaning and purpose into everything that you do. It outlines the unique difference you want to make in your current role at work and/or in life. Engaging with the four components of the solution turbine as outlined below will enable you to make an authentic contribution

The Solution Turbine

This is at the core of the solution turbine. It is pivotal to the other sections. This looks at the practical steps that can be taken to implement a solution focused mindset. It offers techniques for conversation and questioning, as well as a technique to help consciously train our mind to focus on what we can influence.

Future Perfect

This component explores creating a blueprint of your preferred future. By which is meant where and how you would like to see yourself in the future. This component is supported by an extensive body of research. Finally it provides tools to assist you in outlining your own future perfect.

Highlights

This component explores the areas in your life that are already working successfully. It offers tools to use to identify your own strengths and areas of competence and also to recognise times of 'exception' when problems usually encountered are circumnavigated. These can all be harnessed to enable you to authentically work towards your future perfect.

Narrow the Focus

This component explores the research relating to execution, time management and goal setting, which it utilises to create a practical and comprehensive guide so that you can create FOCUS goals. By applying the research available it ensures that you are giving yourself the best chance possible to be more consistently functioning at your optimal level and making an authentic contribution.

> "To survive in organisations today you have to be relentlessly curious."
>
> *Jim Collins*

Being solution focused is the core of the turbine. If you want to make moderate changes look at your behaviours, however if you want to make quantum leaps start with developing a solution focused mindset. This chapter examines practical steps you can take to begin to employ solution focused thinking. It is the first step towards creating your authentic contribution.

Useful Conversations

Solution focused language enables you to communicate in a way that facilitates collaboration, and not competition, with others. It also impacts on the outcomes you achieve by influencing your mindset prior to starting a task. How we talk about ourselves, and the language we use when communicating with others, can greatly impact how we are feeling and the results we achieve. If you play a sport such as golf, listen to yourself next time you are playing. Are you saying to yourself before teeing off 'I hope I don't land my ball in the water' or 'I hope I get it near the hole'? The difference could be one of splashing or landing.

Even the syntax of language can influence a person's emotional response to its content. For example, in English, people often say 'I am depressed'. This takes ownership over the depression, and defines the person through this attribution whilst suggesting that it could be a permanent state. The Irish language is more poetic. In Irish, when people are feeling down they say 'Ta brón orm', which translates as 'there is a sadness upon me'. This difference in composition implies a separation between the person and the sadness thereby also inferring a temporary state.

Frame of Reference

A real hiccup to people understanding each other is our tendency to use our own view and experiences as a blueprint for others to follow. This is 'viewing' issues from our 'own frame of reference'. Wittegenstein stated that 'You only know the question you have asked when you hear the answer you receive.' This insight should be used as a way to stand back from our own way of viewing to understand that of others.

It is very easy to tell if someone is using pessimistic thinking by their use of problem focused language. Here are a few examples you might recognise:

- I always get left with no information.
- Nobody understands me.
- I'll never be able to do it.
- I never have anyone to do anything for me.
- I'll never be able to perform any better.

A serious consequence to frequently using problem focused language is that it quite often turns into a self-fulfilling prophecy (as outlined in Chapter 1).

Solution Focused Questioning

Knowing how to ask the right questions is often much more useful than trying to have all the right answers. Essentially, all that skilled and proficient executive coaches do is ask useful questions while remaining in a not-knowing stance. This may appear simple but it is not easy.

Solution focused questions are carefully crafted so as to open up possibilities and creativity whilst building resilience. Below is an example that shows the difference in results between a solution focused questioning approach and a problem focused questioning approach to a typical time management issue. The statement addressed is

"I can't relax because I have no control over my time. Essentially I want a better work life balance."

Solution Focused Approach	Problem Focused Approach
When do you feel like you have more control of your time?	When is time a problem?
When I take time out on Sunday afternoon and go for a jog before a new week begins.	The week goes by and I feel like I haven't even had a chance to look at what matters most.
So how did you manage it?	So what causes the problem of not being able to have a proper work life balance because of time?
I had space to think of my week ahead and to reflect and consider what were the most important things I wanted to do rather than getting caught up in the whirlwind of the day job.	Work demands, the feeling of working hard and achieving very little.
What else?	So with little time available it makes it difficult for you to have the work life balance you want?
I made a list of all the things I want to achieve during the week and highlighted those to be prioritised over all other tasks. Essentially I find I can be continuously busy during each week but achieve none of my important goals because of the impact of my day job.	Sure does, I'll have to wait for work to ease off at some point and then I can look at my work life balance.

The solution focused conversation leads to a useful exploration of possibilities whilst the problem focused conversation often elaborates on what is wrong and potentially exacerbates it.

Resources:

Read 1001 Solution Focused Questions by Fredricke Bannink

Solution Focused Language Tips

"Words were originally magic and to this day words have retained much of their ancient magical power. By words one person can make another blissfully happy or drive him to despair; by words the teacher conveys knowledge to his pupils, by words the orator carries his audience with him and determines their judgements and decisions. Words provoke affects and are in general the means of mutual influence among men."

Sigmund Freud

Useful language skills for dealing with problems can be learnt from 'Colombo' a long running U.S. television detective series starring Peter Falk. I refer to 'Colombo' as the solution detective as he maintains a state of curiosity which requires him to set aside his own frame of reference, previous experience and expertise. A skill enabling him to solve many complex cases.

- Ask 'How?' and not 'Why?

  Using 'why?' often has the effect of making people shut down as they experience a brain freeze which is sometimes described as an 'emotional hijack'. Often people are not even thinking of how to answer a 'why' question but rather how to get out of what is felt as an intimidating and unpleasant situation.

- Replace 'yes, but' with 'yes, and'

  'Yes, and' typically generates more options. 'Yes, but' shuts down any chance of enhanced creativity and exploring possibilities as using the word 'but' essentially infers 'ignore everything I said before it'.

- Ask 'what else?'

  Once we have asked a useful question we have a tendency to rush on to the next. However it can be extremely beneficial to ask 'what else?' as it quite often leads to the discovery of more solutions to problems.

Try and practice these simply steps and see how it facilitates useful dialogue and conversations with others, not least yourself.

31

Respond v. React

"It's not what happens to you, but how you react to it that matters."

Epictetus (Ancient Greek, Stoic Philosopher)

Being solution focused is a choice and one which benefits your well-being and improves results. As discussed in chapter 2, as humans we are hard wired to be problem focused. There is also a short term comfort in throwing our hands up to Allah and allowing ourselves to believe that life is out of our control. However, the negative aftermath of such a reaction can be enormous and evidently not useful. A lot of inspirational people have made the switch from originally utilising a problem focus. Nelson Mandela was originally very reactive and sought a win-lose relationship with the white governing party in South Africa. It wasn't until his incarceration on Robin Island that he changed to a solution focused mindset. He realised that to achieve his goal for his fellow black people it would take win-win solution focused thinking and the inclusion of all people in South Africa.

Event - Solution Choice - Respond

There has been much written about stimulus-response type behaviour by such thought leaders as psychologist Arnold Lazarus (author of In the Mind's Eye), Stephen Covey (author of The 7 Habits of Highly Effective People) and even as far back to the ancient Greek Stoic philosopher Epictetus. As humans we have the ability to separate the distance between an event and our response. Through freedom of thought we can make choices to behave in a more productive solution focused way, rather than a problem focused one.

Resources:

Watch Serena Williams react in a problem focused way which leads to her being overwhelmed by her emotions and paying a heavy price for it during the semi-finals of the US tennis open in 2009. http://www.youtube.com/watch?v=QbObCBxGosM

People often find it too late in the heat of the moment to employ a solution focused approach. Therefore this thinking must be activated at a pre-event stage. Just like an athlete who undergoes pre-match routines and mental preparation, we too can prepare and practice so as to face into any situation with a solution focused mindset. In doing so we ensure that we select and control our preferred choices more consistently. This is especially useful when entering a conflict situation with already existing high levels of anxiety.

"One evening an old Cherokee told his grandson about a battle that goes on inside people. He said, 'My son, the battle is between two wolves inside us all. One is Evil. It is anger, envy, jealously, sorrow, regret, greed, arrogance, self-pity, guilt, resentment, inferiority, lies, false pride, superiority, and ego. The other is Good. It is joy, peace, love, hope, serenity, humility, kindness, benevolence, empathy, generosity, truth, compassion and faith.'

The grandson thought about it for a minute and then asked his grandfather, 'Which wolf wins?' The old Cherokee simply replied, 'The one you feed."

Old Cherokee Legend

Choose a Solution Tool

Problem focused people **often allow an 'emotional hijack' to cause them to react to an event or situation. I commonly refer to this as the nuclear option.**

Solution focused **people take a moment to press pause and then respond to an event or situation with good levels of impulse control. Identifying a Solution Choice allows you to enhance self-trust and to maintain mutually satisfying relationships with others.**

Try this:

Identify a Solution Choice that worked well for you in the past.

How did you manage it?

Control the Controllables

In every situation, there is a huge number of factors that one can control and many others that one cannot. At times we are all problem focused and waste precious time and energy on the things we cannot control. The diagram below illustrates this point:

> "Do not let what you cannot do interfere with what you can do."
>
> *John Wooden*

Factors you can potentially control, as well as what is already working, lie within your solution triangle and the ones you cannot control (at least currently) lie within your problem triangle. We can train our mind through increased self-awareness to direct our attention on the area we want to. In doing so, we can make our mind an ally and the best tool for coping with problems.

When we are faced with change we use both a solution focus and problem focus. We are hardwired to look at problems which contain our weaknesses and what's broken or not working in our current situation. In many cases it has served us well and made us an evolutionary success story. It is however a prime example of pessimistic attribution theory in action (as outlined in chapter 2). When the caveman set foot outside of his cave he needed such problem focused 'knee jerk' reactions to ensure his survival. However in the 21st century focusing the majority of our time on problems is just that - 'a problem'!

Interestingly, whichever triangle you decide to focus on will expand and consume your valuable time, energy and attention. Your problem triangle is made up of most things that you can do nothing about in the short term. If you spend a lot of your time there it will leave you with an overwhelming sense of a lack of control. During times of added anxiety people often disengage, feeling a sense of 'learned helplessness'. Such people are unwittingly cultivating a problem focus.

Focusing your mind on your solution triangle, no matter how small it may feel at the time, allows you to increase and expand your solution thinking through exploring possibilities while diminishing your problem focus.

Let's use an example from the world of sport. Imagine you are about to take a conversion kick in a big game of rugby. You are more likely to perform at your most optimal and relaxed way if you have your mind focused within your solution triangle, which may include such things as:

• I have practiced for this many times

• I have made such kicks successfully in competition many times

• I have the ability

• I have nothing to lose

• There is always next time

• Sure it'll be grand

Alternatively if you allow your focus to drift predominantly to your problem triangle then your thinking can very easily and quickly become overwhelmed and occasionally lead to an emotional hijack with such thoughts as:

• The crowd is very hostile

• The referee has it in for me

• I've missed at this distance before

• I'll be substituted if I miss

• The wind is picking up

• I didn't sleep well last night

• My team mates are expecting me to miss

Such a problem focus can lead to disastrous results as it can cause an over-reactivity in our nervous system. We have all had the experience of having to complete something new or difficult while others are watching which we know we could complete with far more ease if we were left to our own devices. However, you can perform better more consistently if you train and develop your mind to focus more within your solution triangle, especially in moments of elevated anxiety. At first when you begin to practice this it may seem unnatural or overly formulaic. Nevertheless, over time it will slowly become a part of your psyche and how you think and respond to situations.

When trying out a new skill or trying to develop a new habit 'less is often more'. If I am working with an athlete I don't suggest that they try to utilise this (or other) emotional skills for the first time in their next big match, rather it is important to build skills up slowly. First through mental rehearsal, then in a safe environment such as in training and then eventually on match day - therefore it will be more likely to stick and be a psych skill that is more easily accessible in competition.

To recap, the majority of time when we experience excessive mental chatter and heightened levels of anxiety it is because too much of our emotional energy is being consumed by living within our problem triangle. Change happens where the awareness is and once we become aware of the thoughts that are colonising our mind we can do something positive about it. Use the tool below to do just that.

The Solution Focus Tool

A solution focus consists of what is already working, possible solutions as well as what you have some control over.

- Identify a problem that makes you feel stuck.

- Now brainstorm a list of all the issues associated with it.

① From your list identify five or more possible solutions, what you can control or influence and what is already working that might help you meet the challenge more effectively?

② How do you manage to control each of these things?

③ Identify five or more things about your problem situation that you cannot control in the short term.

Now examine what you have come up with and choose to focus primarily within your solution triangle in dealing with your problem and watch it grow. You can literally apply this method to a plethora of situations including work problems, pre-interview nerves or arranging a romantic date. People who are anxious at night time and find it difficult to sleep are more than likely allowing their mind to overly focus on their problems and all the non-controllable issues associated with them. Many people I have worked with have found that by focusing their minds on 'what's already working' and 'possible solutions' has allowed them to be able to drift soundly off to sleep.

Summary of Chapter 3

→ The solution turbine is a model designed to generate the energy of positive emotion and to unleash the power of positive psychology on to whatever you focus it on.

→ Leaning the art of useful conversations helps you to create the world you want to live in.

→ Enhanced collaboration is made possible through the art of solution focused conversations.

→ We all learn scripts very early on and are conditioned to respond to things in certain ways often unconsciously.

→ Solution focused questions open up possibilities and problem focused questions limit them.

→ Using solution focused self-talk is the direct route to developing an optimistic mindset.

→ Responding to a situation is often more useful than reacting in the moment.

→ Being solution focused is a choice and one which sees us being able to respond rather than to react to situations.

→ Solution focused individuals seek out possibilities whereas problem focused people tend to get bogged down by things they currently have little or no control over.

4 Future Perfect

Chapter outline

One day, before Jim Carrey became a celebrated Hollywood actor, he went up to the famous Hollywood sign overlooking Los Angeles with a clearly defined future perfect in mind. He wrote himself a post-dated cheque for millions of dollars which he duly cashed years later.

Research supports the maxim that communicating to others or writing down a goal makes it much more likely to happen be it running a marathon or losing a few pounds.

"The best way to predict the future is to create it."

Peter Drucker

U2 singer Bono took inspiration from the poet William Butler Yeats who often wrote from the perspective of being dead. This approach, Yeats believed, freed up his mind, opening it to possibilities of literary creativity. When you take the time to imagine your own future perfect and to think about the legacy you would like to leave behind, it creates a space for creative thinking towards your end goals.

Why do you work? The usual answer I hear to this is 'to get paid'. Over 30 years of research proves that the biggest motivating factor for people being highly

engaged in work is not money. Interestingly, once people believe that they are being paid fairly, giving them further excessive bonuses does little to increase their motivation. What the research indicates 'works best' is for people to feel that they are making an authentic contribution and that their lives, and indeed, work contain a strong sense of purpose.

"It is impossible to have a great life unless it is a meaningful life."

Jim Collins

One obstacle I often encounter when asking future perfect questions is that people state 'I will have won the lotto or got a promotion' and so on. If you are tempted to answer in a similar fashion, ask yourself another useful question - what would you be doing differently then that you are not doing now? (i.e. once you have won the lotto or got a promotion). Interestingly, most people list things that they could actually bring into their lives in some shape or form right now.

Strangely, some people make a 'bucket list' of all the things that they would most like to do or accomplish when they feel their life is coming to an end. Similarly most of us invest money and much thought in ensuring our life insurance policies and pensions are in place, and would consider it foolhardy not to do so. It seems commonplace to plan for the end of our lives and our deaths. However, far less of us invest as much time in making a plan for living.

If you value something and it is not in your life in some shape or form right now - what is the point? Do you remember being good at something when you were younger? Everyone probably said how you were brilliant at football, poetry or with numbers and so on. What happens to the majority of us is that we often over rely on our obvious talent with a sense of inner confidence that it will get us through life. Most likely as we go through our twenties nothing much happens, then into our thirties and still no sign! When suddenly BANG we have a midlife crisis as we come to the realisation that 'nobody is coming to rescue us' - this is the danger of not having a future perfect outlined for every important goal you have.

"What you expect to happen influences what you do."

Steve de Shazer

The Paradox of Choice

In today's world the abundance of choices often causes people to disengage and act as if they are waiting for their real life to come around the corner and hit them like a religious conversion. Creating a detailed description of our future perfect, acts as a blueprint to our personal vision. This blueprint of our preferred future not only includes where we want to be but also who we are and/or would like to be, which allows us to grow. It also ignites recognition of our ability to have control over making a positive impact on ourselves and the world around us. Creating a future perfect allows us to live holistically in the way we want to live so that we are not just 'doing things' for a living but rather so that we are living authentically (by being solution focused).

Outlining your future perfect gives you a strong drive to achieve personally meaningful goals. You will be energised by the stimulus of pushing yourself outside of your comfort zone to take on new challenges. A future perfect gives you more of a passion for what you do. A future perfect embodies a process that allows you to throw your rucksack over a wall and to commit yourself to something bigger than yourself or what you are doing currently. As Oscar Wilde famously commented 'We are all in the gutter but some of us our looking at the stars.' and that's a solution focus.

In short, creating a future perfect . . .

- Clarifies what we would like from the future

- Fills us with positive emotion

- Takes us away from being problem focused

- Gives us a sense of hope

- Increases our resilience

- Strengthens neurological muscles

- Decreases stress

- Increases psychological well being

RESOURCE: Martin Luther King made clear his future perfect through his 'I have a dream' speech. View it on www.youtube.com for inspiration before writing your own shortly.

Future Perfect Examples:

My Future Perfect:

In my future perfect I will be making a positive difference. I will seek to understand what my family and my vocational strengths are and how they can be made to flourish, so everyone can feel strong and confident. I will seek out the creation of contagious happiness, laughter and positive emotion as we journey through life together. I will seek to be myself with more skill on a daily basis. I will be comfortable not being an expert or someone who possesses absolute truths or answers whilst being a comfort by sharing this with others. I will be authentic, non-judgemental, courageous, appreciative and a free spirit.

Another Example:

To laugh often and much

to win the respect of
intelligent people

and the affection of children;

to earn the appreciation of
honest critics

and endure the betrayal of
false friends;

to appreciate beauty;

to find the best in others;

to leave the world a bit
better,

whether by a healthy child,

a garden patch

or a redeemed social
condition;

to know even one life has
breathed easier

because you have lived.

This *is to have succeeded.*

Poem by Ralph Waldo Emerso

Future Perfect Tool

The following eight questions
have been designed to get you
ready to explore your own future
perfect. When answering, do not
worry about having a strategy for
how to put your future perfect
into action at this stage as that
can get in the way of the flow of
positive emotion and creativity.

Step 1: Useful Future Perfect Exploration Questions

1. If time and expense weren't an issue I would . . .

2. If I truly wasn't afraid I would . . .

3. If I won the lottery what I would be doing differently would be . . .

4. If I worked within my solution triangle and outside of my job description, I would . . .

5. What conversations will your friends and family be having at your funeral? What songs will they be singing that remind them of you?

6. What will people be saying about you when you have arrived at your future perfect?

7. What legacy do you want to leave?

8. If you were the person your dog thinks you are what would you be doing differently?

Step 2: Write your future perfect statement: What do you want to achieve in your life?

This second step encourages you to create an emotional resonance with your future perfect by capturing your heart, mind and wallet.

View, enjoy, dissect and digest what you have written. Are there any re-emerging themes that could make a difference to your life? Summarise in your own way (e.g. pictures, charts, mind-mapping, speech bubbles, shapes, words, quotations):

Summary of Chapter 4

→ A future perfect is a blueprint for life.

→ In today's world there is a paradox of choice in that we have more options than ever available, however many achieve less with more.

→ Get rid of the noise and attention paid to the less important things in life which often consume most of our time.

→ A well crafted future perfect instills meaning and purpose into your life.

→ Research shows that sharing and communicating your future perfect makes it increasingly more likely to happen.

→ Do not sit back and wait for your purpose in life to come around the corner and hit you in the head like a religious conversion.

→ The future perfect application tool is designed to help you write a compelling future perfect statement.

Highlights

5

Chapter outline

→ Living Highlights
→ Positive Ticketing
→ Positive Deviance
→ In Search of Exceptions
→ Strengths
→ No Time like Flow Time

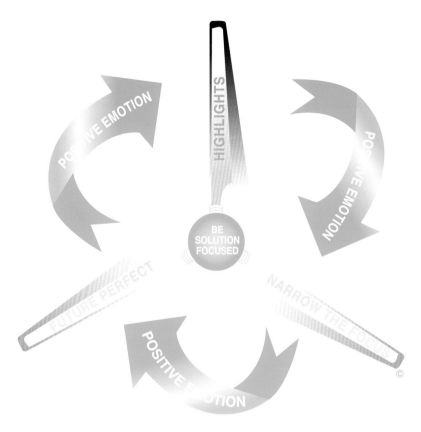

"Awards are funny...you win one you think
you are brilliant and if you lose you think
you are crap and neither is true."

Sinead O'Connor,
Winner of An Irish Meteor Music Award 2008

Living Highlights

This blade of the turbine unleashes a person's self-esteem and confidence. A 'Highlight' encapsulates your personal strengths and what you are doing when things are working well in your life.

In this chapter we will be shining a spotlight on the areas of your life where things are already working well. By embracing a solution focused approach we will analyse what you are already doing effectively, as well as what is happening when a problem is lessened. Fundamentally, your success is likely to depend more on you doing better the things you already know how to do. Performance often varies dramatically as people often fail to analyse adequately what works, and when it does, what strengths they are utilising and what they are doing differently at that time.

"There is nothing wrong with you that what is right can't fix."

Insoo Kim Berg

Once you have a clearer understanding of these positives already at work they can be harnessed as you journey towards your future perfect. It is this awareness that will allow you to create clear goals that will help you make your authentic contribution. Your abilities and previous successful experiences will help you reach your future perfect.

Positive Ticketing

The 'positive ticketing' idea started with a single police officer who had a simple idea in mind for his future perfect - 'Imagine cops catching kids doing things right!' The initiation of positive ticketing started within the Royal Canadian Mounted Police. It grew out of a history of distrust between the police force and young adults. Most interactions were of a negative nature and only reinforced the distance between them. The crime rate was also increasing. The police force was left fighting fires and reacting to situations rather than taking any preventative measures, until that is, they introduced positive ticketing.

The police force started to give youths who were exemplifying desirable behaviour rewards in the form of positive tickets. The positive tickets are rewards in the form of vouchers or tokens for goods or services. These tickets range from a complementary entrance to the local cinema, a takeaway pizza, admittance to a fun park, pitch and putt or swimming pool. The idea is simple, rather than a youth cycling on public streets without wearing a helmet and being worried about receiving a ticket as punishment the police officers concern themselves with finding and positively ticketing the youths who are wearing helmets or who are rollerblading on the right side of the footpath and so on. Catching kids doing the right things also helps the police's morale and resilience levels. Most importantly the police report that it opens a relationship gateway to help them connect with the youth. It also saves the taxpayer money as there is a huge decrease in the costs associated with dealing with youth crime.

The police also noticed a more united approach with local business who are providing free activities to be included as part of the ticketing scheme. Another benefit is a better public image for the police. Through their interaction with youths the police are helping to improve educational outcomes; which in turn leads to better employment opportunities. The results speak for themselves - The City of Richmond, British Columbia, Canada experienced an amazing 41% reduction in their youth crime over three years, in which, they claim, positive ticketing was a major contributing factor. The idea is spreading fast. There are pilot initiatives happening all over the world, with the latest interest coming from Sydney, Australia.

Similarly, certain enlightened schools have teachers who understand the benefit of 'catching kids doing the right thing'. They do this in one way by highlighting what a student answers correctly rather than handing them back their work full of red marks and expecting them to feel inspired or believe they have potential. The rationale is that students learn and get more out of focusing on what they get right as opposed to 'wrong'. They will know which areas they are weak in. However they are more likely to be eager to improve and do better starting from a strengths based approach

by focusing on what they can do. The more traditional approach is quite often responsible for the development of 'learned helplessness' in children.

Resources:

Watch 'Lil' Nikki' - Akwasasne Mohawk School Police Officer, Constable Nicole Miller, explain the 'Positive Ticket' program she runs with the local youth. www.youtube.com/watch?v=9ZjHtrPNQu8

For more examples of positive ticketing and case studies visit: www.positiveticketing.com

Positive Deviance

Positive deviance is a community driven problem solving approach which focuses on successes and puts an action plan together for all to join. It originated with the Save the Children Foundation* where it was found to be highly effective at such things as combating child malnutrition in over 41 countries worldwide to enhancing child retention levels in primary schools in Argentina.

* Save the Children is a charity whose mission is to inspire breakthroughs in the way the world treats children, and to achieve immediate and lasting change in their lives.

Let's look at an example

In 1991 children in Vietnam were experiencing widespread malnutrition (at a level of 65%). However what was surprising was that some children were not suffering malnutrition even though they were living in similar dire conditions with the same level of resources available to them as those that were. Interestingly, the children who were not suffering from malnutrition were positive deviants. How come? Because they were deviating in their behaviours from what the majority of others were doing and it was having a powerful positive impact. What were they doing differently? The children were being fed more frequently and with less food. Their parents were also collecting shrimp and crabs from paddy fields and adding it to their children's meals along with sweet potato greens. This was food which was traditionally considered only suitable for adults to consume.

Identifying positive deviants helps highlight solutions that are already working and are a good fit culturally, rather than utilising a more traditional 'off the shelf' solution which is likely to have limited success in terms of timing and longevity. Furthermore the Vietnamese government realised that the results achieved by traditional supplemental feeding programs were rarely maintained after the programs ended.

The highlight blade takes a positive deviance outlook by helping you to do more of the actions that make you feel strong and help you make an authentic contribution towards your future perfect.

It is possible to do this by focusing on what you are doing differently when a problem is lessened or the road blocks stopping you making your authentic contribution are not as powerful or obvious. Fundamentally, your success is likely to depend more on you doing better the things you already know how to do rather than on launching into listing major problems which are holding you back from making an authentic contribution. As previously mentioned performance often varies dramatically as people fail to analyse adequately what works and, when it does, what they are doing differently at the time.

Your quest is to move beyond the mindset of doing what is required towards a mindset of making a real contribution which will make a real difference. If you want to see the power of positive deviance at work you will want to do the following:

- Identify islands of excellence - when are you behaving in ways aligned to your future perfect and what positive deviant activities are you involved in at the time?

Think for a moment of the islands of excellence that exist within your organisation or football team and so on. What behaviours are the positive deviants involved in which are having a positive impact. Now move the core of the people (i.e. the majority) to join them by modelling the mindset and behaviours of the outliers. Coincidentally, the more often you do this the more you will start to recognise them. It is worth noting that the majority of people want to move or make a difference but a lot of the time they are unsure of how to do it. A recent Gallup poll stated that 49% of people did not know how what they were doing in their day to day job contributed to the overall goal of their organisation. Think about it, how hard do you play if no one is keeping score or indeed knows how to? If you play against me in a game of tennis and we are not keeping score it is more likely to turn into a 'knock around' rather than a competitive match which exploits our true strengths.

Resources:

If you would like to read more inspirational positive deviance stories or to get involved in a positive deviant initiative visit www.positivedeviance.org.

In order to establish what is already successfully occurring we will be doing the following:

- Identifying exceptions to problems
- Identifying your strengths

In Search of Exceptions

"No problem exists all the time, at least to the same intensity."

Steve de Shazer

There are exceptions to everything and every problem. Analysing these exceptions and what is going on when they are happening can help illuminate possibilities as to what might solve the problem. Let me illustrate an example of exception seeking: When someone says that they are completely depressed - you could ask 'Has there being a time over the last while when you weren't depressed?'

'What was happening then?'

'How did you manage to cope?'

Exceptions Tool:

In the previous chapter we outlined a desired future perfect. With it in mind, try answering the following:

- Have there been times when you have had a sense of your future perfect in your life already, say in the last three months?

- If so what was happening at the time?

- What is it about the identified exception that might be useful to remember as you journey towards your future perfect?

Wittgenstein wrote: 'The aspects of things that are most important for us are hidden because of their simplicity and familiarity' as essentially one is unable to notice something - because it is always before one's eyes.

So ask yourself . . .

- What would need to happen to allow you to make these exceptions a more permanent state?

Remember identifying exceptions shines a spotlight on potentially untapped or indeed unconscious resources and focusing on them allows us to access already available solutions and strategies that can be built on.

Strengths

"The enemy of the great is the good."

Voltaire

Essentially the curse of mediocrity drives us to spend too much time trying to improve within areas that are not areas of strength for us. A problem focus typically ignores strengths and hones in on weaknesses. At best a weakness can be worked on to become an average strength, so why not invest this energy into finding and developing your true strengths? This is where you can make the most difference. At the end of the day one of your weaknesses will be somebody else's strength, so why not leave it to them and vice versa?

In 2008 Brian O'Driscoll captained the Irish rugby team that went into the world cup in France that year as a firm favourite. They had a terrible tournament and O'Driscoll's game appeared to suffer shortly afterwards. He made the following comment when interviewed by Sky News. 'The big thing that I got this year came from a sport's psychologist: "practice the things you are good at". People always practice what they are poor at. There were times at the start of the season when I was just in bad form; my confidence was low; you just have to get out of the rut and look at the good things you can do and are good at. Sometimes you need to replay old footage of you doing good things and remind yourself that you haven't lost those things overnight.'

I also know of an extremely successful golfer who works hard at improving her game. Her swing is legendary and her putting is exemplary (though not quite as good as her swing). You might then expect her to invest most of her practice time on her putting. However she doesn't. In fact she only allocates 20% of her time to her putting whilst 80% of her time she spends on her swing. It is the thing that she does better than most people. She has also commented that working on her strengths leaves her feeling more relaxed, energised, focused and confident.

Similarly, Denis Rodman who used to play basket ball for the Chicago Bulls capitalised on his strengths creatively. He loved rebounding and in fact some might say that he turned it into an art form. "I rebound with a little flair, a little something extra," stated Rodman. "It's not for the crowd; it's just for me. Rebounding is how I express myself on the floor."

There is a significant amount of research which shows that people who can clearly identify and utilise their strengths also experience enhanced levels of wellbeing and optimal functioning.

Know Your Strengths Tool:

1. What job related activities give you a buzz?

2. When are you in a flow state?

3. What would you continue doing even if you weren't being paid?

4. As a child you knew instinctively what you enjoyed and what made you feel strong. What was it?

5. What job related activities have you done that have allowed you to play to your strengths or excited you?

6. What do you read? What interests you?

7. How would your manager, colleagues and people who know you well answer the previous questions in relation to you?

"Learning happens where the awareness is."

Timothy Galloway

Strengths are not simply something you are good at, these are competencies. A lot of people get stuck working in areas of competencies because more than likely someone identified it as an area of strength for them. However it is only an area of strength if it is something that makes you feel strong. Of course competencies quite often are strengths, but not always, and that is why you might be frustrated or unhappy working in an area that you are particularly good at (or you could be good at if you wanted to be.)

Tool: Strength or Competence Finder

Marcus Buckingham (author of Go Put Your Strengths to Work) carried out extensive research into understanding the difference between strengths and competencies and has developed a strength test called SIGN which I will outline below. How you answer these questions in relation to an activity will be a good indicator as to whether you are looking at a personal strength or a competence.

Success: Is it something I have always excelled at?

Instinct: Am I instinctively passionate about it - is it a gut feel?

Growth: Is it an area which has me thinking of all kinds of possibilities for it on a regular basis?

Need: Does it satisfy a need for me, and is it an activity which I recall fondly and look forward to in the future?

If you answer 'yes' to these questions then it is a strength. If not, then perhaps it is an area of competence, talent and skill but not strength.

No Time like Flow Time

Another way in which a differentiation can be made between strengths and competencies is that strengths are things that make you feel strong, creative, confident and give you the feeling of being in a flow state, whereby you are functioning at your optimal level. Understanding how to recognise when you are in a flow state can also be used as a tool to identify your strengths.

Flow is a mental state in which a person is fully immersed in an activity that gives them a feeling of energised focus where time just seems to pass freely. It has been described as a euphoric high or an out of body experience, which typically leaves the person feeling refreshed but tired.

Psychologist Mihaly Csíkszentmihályi (author of Finding Flow: The Psychology of Engagement with Everyday Life) developed a flow model which illustrates the mental state necessary to achieve flow moments in terms of challenge and skill levels.

Elite athletes know how to frequently tap into flow states. As the model illustrates you need to perfectly align the balance between your skill (i.e. ability) and the level of challenge of what you attempting to accomplish. If you are far superior to me at snooker you are unlikely to experience a flow moment when playing against me as your better skill will lead to boredom. Conversely, if you play someone who is far superior to you and the challenge is too much you are also unlikely to experience a flow state as you will be experiencing heightened levels of anxiety.

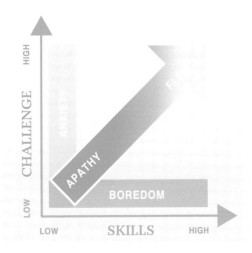

Flow Activity

Think of a moment in sport, at home, a hobby, a social interaction or something you did recently that you did well, and that you enjoyed doing. A time you felt in the flow, confident and alive. Once you have identified one, answer the following questions:

1 How were you able to do it?

2 What else?

3 What did you do to make it happen?

4 Knowing yourself as you do what strengths and qualities were you tapping into?

5 If you recognised and had these flow moments more frequently and consistently, what would you notice?

6 What would others that know you well notice?

7 If these qualities were to play an even greater part in your life at work, what would you notice?

Of course you may not initially be able to spend your whole day in a flow state or playing to your strengths but you can increase the likelihood by being aware of your strengths and by seeking to make the most of your 'day' or 'work' play to them. Organisations often exclaim that 'our people are our greatest asset'. This is simply not true - employees are not an organisations greatest asset, their strengths are. It is their strengths that allow them to be focused, engaged, resilient and capable of making an authentic contribution. Organisations with supposedly great people may just have a cabinet full of great CVs unless their people are allowed to frequently play to their strengths.

RESOURCE: Martin Seligman's website www. authentichappiness.com allows you to take a complementary assessment that highlights your signature strengths which you will find useful as you read on to discover how you can best realise them.

Using your strengths will give you greater vitality, energy, focus and a sense of optimal well-being, allowing you to flourish. You will also be at less risk of suffering from anxiety, self-doubt and burnout. A solution focused approach to your strengths encourages you to find what works for you rather than trying to recreate or reinvent a different you instead of the 'real you'.

As already mentioned change and learning happens where the awareness is. Therefore realising our strengths requires us to highlight them and that in turn builds them. Simply put - awareness of them helps to develop them as well as re-igniting any latent ones. Remember you will not end up good at all things and neither should that be your ultimate goal, as it will more likely lead to a life of mediocrity. You should take a heat-seeking missile approach to identifying your strengths as opposed to a machine gun one. Playing to your strength allows you to be authentic as it is about being yourself more with skill which also encompasses a feeling of contentment.

Summary of Chapter 5

→ A highlight shines a light on the change you want to see so you can amplify it.

→ Examining highlights enables the full utilisation of your strengths.

→ It is important to seek out exceptions, where problems are surmounted or their intensity lessened.

→ It is vital for continued high performance to know the difference between your strengths and competencies.

→ Being aware of what conditions create flow moments substantially increases the likelihood of you experiencing more of them.

→ It is unrealistic to make your whole life play to your strengths, however with careful design you can make most of it do so!

Part 1 of 2
Narrow the Focus

Chapter outline
PART 1 OF 2

→ Time in a Matrix
→ A Sense of Urgency
→ Solution Focused Execution
→ Say No to SMART Goals

"Things which matter most must never be at the mercy of things which matter least."

Johann Goethe

This blade of the turbine increases a person's level of flexibility. By narrowing the focus you will learn practical ways to work towards your future perfect. This chapter details the research related to change and goal setting. It then harnesses this information into a comprehensive five step tool so that you can create your own goals for working towards your future perfect. This is the fourth step towards creating your authentic contribution.

Time in a Matrix

To provide ourselves with the space to do something different we can benefit from becoming acutely aware of how we are currently managing our time, and then ask ourselves 'Are we spending enough time on what matters most?' Traditional time management and effectiveness programmes frequently use the Eisenhower Matrix (named after the President) which is also referred to as the Time Matrix by Stephen Covey. The process is a useful starting point to develop awareness around where and how we manage our time. Most people keep 'busy busy' because it makes them feel productive. However, they have no idea whether 'what they are doing' or indeed 'how they are doing it' is the most productive method for them.

"Never confuse movement with action."

Ernest Hemmingway

Below is a version of the popular matrix. It is a useful way to enhance awareness of where currently our time is mainly concentrated.

	URGENT	NOT URGENT
IMPORTANT	• Unexpected crises • Unforeseen meetings • Pressing issues • Various demands • Surprise deadlines **1**	• Solution focused work • Preparation • Prevention • Future perfect blueprint • Mind mapping • Networking • FOCUS goals • Living highlights **2**
NOT IMPORTANT	• Senseless interruptions • Unnecessary meetings • Unimportant reports • Other people concerns • Indiscriminate emails, phone calls & texts **3**	• Busy rather than focused work • Irrelevant phone calls & email • Time wasting procrastination • Pleasant activities carried out excessively **4**

The matrix is made up of the following four quadrants:

Number 2: is the 'Not urgent' but 'Important' quadrant which I refer to as the quadrant of authenticity. It infuses balance and allows you to look at what will enable you 'to be yourself more with skill'. It contains such things as your values, planning, preparation, an authentic contribution, goals, a future perfect blueprint, exploring highlights and relationship building. It is important - in fact it should be labelled as extremely important. However, the activities do not have an urgency attached to them. Interestingly this quadrant is called 'Not Urgent' when really there is nothing more urgent than ensuring you are living authentically. If neglected it falls foul of the same failing to plan or prioritise that leads to people having to resort to using a bucket list. Examine this quadrant and you will see it contains all the ideas and activities that instantly make sense and that we can all identify with. However it is also the area that we are always going to get around to when we have the time or can 'press pause' for long enough. The more time we spend in this quadrant ultimately assists us with dealing more effectively with the fire-fighting that continuously happens in the following Quadrant.

Number 1: is the 'Urgent' and 'Important' quadrant and which I refer to as the quadrant of Now! It possesses an intoxicating addictiveness. It is the 'go go' whirlwind that consumes you the minute you roll out of bed each morning. It is normally what you are being paid to do or other important responsibilities. It contains pressing issues, unexpected crises and project driven activities. It is possible to spend a significant amount of your time in this quadrant, and still carry out what is required for you to make an authentic contribution. The popularity of this quadrant is garnered from the fact that we are evolutionarily hard wired for urgency. However it does leave you with less time to spend in what is considered the most productive quadrant (i.e. quadrant number 2) as well as the feeling of being burnt out. The problem with persistent adrenaline highs is that what goes up must come down. However no matter what you do, you will always have to spend a significant amount of time within quadrant number 1 out of necessity.

Number 3: is the 'Not Important' but 'Urgent' quadrant which I refer to as the quadrant of noise. People in this quadrant are quick to tell you how swamped they are and how there isn't enough hours in the day. This quadrant should really be labelled 'Appears Urgent' as these pressing issues are likely to be urgent, but for someone else. It is quite a deceptive quadrant, especially in terms of how much time people seem to spend contributing to other people's goals at the expense of their own. It contains such things as other people's concerns, as well as their low and high priorities, the meeting you attend with no real purpose (for you) and excessive needless interruptions. It leaves you with the same feeling that answering all unwanted letters and spam mail would do. Whenever anyone tells me they simply do not have the time to implement an authentic contribution towards their future perfect, I point out that there is always time to be taken back from quadrant number 3. Unless you have clearly defined a strong authentic contribution to be made towards a future perfect you are likely to fall victim to this quadrant, busily working away towards other people's goals and nowhere towards developing your own future perfect. You can arrive at work each morning without a goal in your head and still be busy all day long with quadrant number 3 activities.

Number 4: is the 'Not Important' and 'Not Urgent' quadrant which I refer to as the quadrant of anxiety because if you spend a considerable of amount of time within it you soon feel little movement or positive progress is ever made in your life. This quadrant might sound quite relaxing and it might be for short periods of time, but really this quadrant is about activities carried out to excess. It contains such things as excessive internet usage or relentlessly playing game consoles. These activities are then anything but relaxing, because rather than you being in control they are controlling you. Remember change is stressful when it appears unpredictable and uncontrollable. Various experiments have proven that television channel hopping often leaves people in a state of mild depression. I might be seeing a counselling client who will divulge that they have no idea why they are feeling bad as they took the previous day off work to relax. When I enquire how they spent their time relaxing, quite often they tell me that they spent the majority of the time watching unselected television programmes.

Have you got a sense of how much time you spend in each quadrant? Ask yourself what impact would it make if you took the focus and energy that you put into quadrant 1, 3 & 4 and primarily put it into quadrant 2?

A Sense of Urgency

As mentioned I find traditional productivity methods such as the Eisenhower or the Time Matrix a useful place to start as an insight into how we utilise our time. However, I have also found that understanding the matrix alone does not make a quadrant number 2 lifestyle more readily accessible to people with any great degree of consistency, as quite simply it doesn't stick. Having this awareness is an excellent first step, however daily life often swamps our well intentioned aims unless there is a plan. Solution focused execution is required to bring a sense of urgency and focus to the all important quadrant number 2 activities. You will find solution focused execution invaluable to implementing the authentic contribution you want to make towards your future perfect.

Solution Focused Execution

Solution focused execution is a commitment to oneself in the form of a personal contract for change. Knowledge without action is often pretty much useless - indeed everything you have read so far in the book is unlikely to come to fruition without it.

Research shows that over 70% of change initiatives fail. Solution focused execution will increase your chances dramatically of not being part of the 70% statistic.

Lack of clarity is the main reason people often appear to resist change. However, what appears to be resistance is often uncertainty about what to do and where to start! Put simply, trying to attain your future perfect can appear daunting and quite overwhelming without narrowing the focus.

Say No to SMART Goals

People generally use SMART goals (i.e. specific, measurable, attainable, realistic & time bound) and they are an extremely popular way to create targets, but not as useful when dealing with behavioural change. They work better if you have a clearly defined outcome as SMART goals assume motivation, however they don't create it. A SMART goal is useful if you want to achieve specific activities but is less useful when looking to change a person. A future perfect contains aspirations, legacies, values and contributions yet to be made - not a figure like wanting a certain percentage return on equity. Further support for this is garnered from change management experts Kotter and Cohen who state that analytical tools work better when 'parameters are known, assumptions are minimal, and the future is not fuzzy.' To take a solution focused approach to goal setting we use the FOCUS execution tool as pictured in part 2 on page 72.

Summary of Part 1 of Chapter 6

→ An awareness of effective time management skills is not enough as knowledge without practice is often futile.

→ The majority of people who try something new fail and this is quite often because they do not bring a sense of urgency to what it is they are trying to achieve.

→ Solution focused execution is a commitment to oneself in the form of a personal contract for change.

→ A SMART goal is useful if you want to achieve specific activities but less so if you are trying to work on behavioural change.

6

Part 2 of 2
Narrow the Focus

Chapter outline
PART 2 OF 2

→ **F** ew in Number (crafting solution focused goals)
→ **O** urselves (goal alignment)
→ **C** hunks (shrink the change)
→ **U** se Scaling (keeping score)
→ **S** imple (keep it simple)

FOCUS Execution Tool

F.O.C.U.S. Execution Tool

F
Few in Number

Choose only 2-3 goals at a time if you want to increase the likelihood of achieving them with excellence.

O
Ourselves

These goals are for you. Everybody's future perfect and highlights are different, so make sure you align your goals with yours. This makes them easier to sustain as you are doing what comes to you naturally and authentically.

C
Chunks

Break down your goals into doauble chunks. To do this, use the following simple formula: From X to Y by When.

U
Use Scaling

Keeping score is a great way of keeping up motivation especially in hard moments. This enables you to look back at what has already been achieved to aid impetus as well as having a tangible next step to achieve.

S
Simple

Keep it simple. Simple language and simple goals are more impactful – as Einstein stated *"everything should be made simple but no simpler"*

Focus

1. Few in Number

As the comedian Billy Connolly says too many instructions during sex is a killer as: 'I can't concentrate'.

So what is a solution focused execution approach to goals and how does it differ?

Do one (to three) things differently

Quite often, even the most seemingly simple activity such as food shopping can be mentally draining because of the amount of options available. This is because the number of options available impacts negatively on our decision making capabilities. It literally causes 'decision paralysis' which leads us to undertake no action, or at best to make some decisions but none with excellence. Interestingly, the average life span of a C.E.O. within a Top Fortune 500 company is only 18 months. Why you may ask? Quite simply they tend to take on too many goals in order to get the job in the first place. Their work load is unrealistic and the commitments they have made to various stakeholders are impossible to deliver on.

Tony Schwartz wrote an interesting book called The Paradox of Choice. He outlines how we all crave 'choice' and indeed one of the highest valued principles of the western world is the freedom of choice. Interestingly however, too much choice can be overwhelming and actually damaging. Schwartz's research illustrates 'why more is less' and how the culture of abundance robs us of satisfaction. My mother-in-law recently received a phone call from her bank trying to sell her a mobile phone and holiday insurance. Her feedback when asked what she would like from her bank was 'I would like my bank to be a bank!' - A good illustration of this point.

There is a danger of having too many goals and taking a machine-gun like approach. The table below contains some interesting findings from research into the number of goals likely to be achieved with excellence in relation to the number of goals set.

Number of Goals	2 - 3	4 - 6	7 - 11
Goals Achieved with Excellence	2 - 3	1 - 2	0

As you can see 'the law of diminishing returns' comes into play quite dramatically. The key message is to take on only a few new goals and remember that these are in addition to what you are expected to achieve already. When I am working with an athlete I often ask them what new activities they are going to try between now and our next session. I get apprehensive when they list off numerous goals because quite simply they are taking on too much. Then, on match day, this scattered approach results in their new activities or psych skills failing to work. Consequently, they will blame themselves, me, psychology or something - it doesn't really matter. The bottom line is that they have failed to recognise how less is more, and as the old Chinese proverb states, 'if you want to go fast go slow'. This is especially true when you are trying out new things.

So far we have examined certain applications behind how to make a solution focused execution plan. With this in mind it is now possible to use this information to create your own carefully crafted solution focused goals towards your future perfect.

Solution Focused Goals Example:

If my future perfect involved setting up a new company my solution focus goals might initially contain the following three goals:

1. Complete business plan by March of this year (i.e. from 30% to 100% by March).

2. Carry out a feasibility study by April of this year.

3. Design website content by May of this year.

Revisit your future perfect statement on page 45 and identify the current 2-3 most important goals that will allow you to make the biggest impact in progressing towards your future perfect? (i.e. if these goals are not accomplished then nothing else matters).

fOCus

2. Ourselves

Key to implementing our future perfect is ensuring that we are creating goals that are tailored to ourselves. This starts with developing greater self-awareness. It is often easy to identify a solution to a certain problem. The goal could be as simple as to get fit. Initially, you might think 'this is a straightforward goal' but then nothing happens. First you need to explore what approach to fitness works best for you.

Goals like wanting to be healthier, or telling your business team to be more creative or to 'focus' are unlikely to stick or be durable. For real change you would need to list what healthier looks like for you, for example 'no food after 8 pm' or to explain what you expect the team to achieve when they are more focused. Essentially, clarify in greater granularity the expressions that you are using. So for example, if as a team member you receive feedback that you need to be more 'switched on' during meetings consider what would be different when you are more 'switched on' for example you might be 'asking more clarifying questions', 'talking straight', 'practicing accountability' and/or 'regularly checking for understanding'.

FOCus

3. CHUNKS: Shrink the Change/Small Wins

"If you want to change big things, you pay attention to small things."

Rudy Guiliani

A well-known example of a successful execution of goals is Rudy Guiliani's zero tolerance approach when he was mayor of New York City. A 2001 study of New York City (NYC) crime trends saw a dramatic fall in petty and serious crime and indeed it was to drop year on year after that for 10 years. The work towards this started in the nineties when the police were desperately trying to "clean up" the streets in NYC and make them safe and welcoming for both the people who lived there and tourists alike. The success lay in seeking to make small changes which led to a ripple effect of positive change, rather than seeking to arrive at a future perfect overnight. It stemmed from 'the broken window theory' which was first put forward by James Wilson and George Kelling. Simply put 'small crime' left unattended causes others to add to it. The City's approach was both simple and clever. They focused on smaller crimes - a broken window left unfixed led to people having less respect for the city and this led to more unwanted behaviour. So city officials started to focus on the small things they could do such as implementing a zero-tolerance approach to fare-dodging, public drinking, urination, and the 'squeegee men' who harassed people by wiping their car windows. These small steps led to a big change and improvement in people's quality of life in NYC. This approach can be used in most aspects of life - from relatively small goals such as getting fit to implementing strategic career changes.

The Progress Principle

In 2011 Harvard Business School Professors Teresa Amabile and Steven Kramer published a book outlining their research findings into the 'progress principle' -which looked at how to use 'small wins' to ignite joy, engagement, and creativity at work. Their research shows how making forward progress towards something you find meaningful is a huge motivator. They discuss the power of 'small wins' in developing positive emotion. A problem focus can have the opposite impact and be a de-railer as it often leads to a feeling of learned helplessness.

Interestingly the negative impact of having a setback is two to three times stronger than that of a positive impact, so it is important to avoid minor de-railers. To do this you must harness the power of 'small wins' and progress. As with solution focused execution the most important thing they found was the need to focus. They suggest that to make significant progress towards the work that is most important and meaningful to you, you should spend at least half an hour a day working on it. It is also useful to keep track of small wins and progress (on a scale board which we will look at next). The progress principle also emphasises the need for clear goals as well as acknowledging the importance of a clearly defined 'future perfect' as a big motivator.

To return to an example used earlier, that of Roger Bannister's breaking of the 4-minute mile in 1954. Bannister 'shrunk the change' by breaking down his goal into small steps. Similarly successful athletes with strong mental toughness primarily focus on performance goals i.e. what they can do (authentic contribution) rather than on outcome goals (future perfect).

FOCUS

4. Use Scaling:

Your future perfect becomes less useful if it appears and feels too daunting and overwhelming. So we shrink the change by using a solution focus tool called scaling. This allows us to find out what is already working so that we can do more of it which keeps us progressing towards our future perfect. As mentioned earlier, scaling makes our goals measureable.

Scaling helps to shrink the change into do-able chunks by identifying small signs of progress (i.e. steps), which builds self-efficacy and therefore increases the likelihood of success. Interestingly, research shows that people are reluctant to donate to charity when the target seems very high as it appears too difficult to accomplish and people feel that their donations will make little or no difference. Many charities are well aware of this and only commence high profile marketing activities when they are well along the journey to success - normally when they have collected at least 50% of what is needed.

The same consumer psychology is being used all around us on a daily basis. Take coffee shop loyalty cards which give you some complimentary stamps towards a free cup of coffee. The coffee houses know you are more likely to return to their coffee shop if you feel your progress towards a free cup of coffee is already under way. Usually it is the power of perceptions at play. The coffee shop next door could have a card system with the same amount of stamps left to collect, however, with no free ones to start you off it feels like your free cup of coffee is a longer way off.

Scaling both measures and enables progress by addressing 'what is already working' and what would be useful to 'do more of'. It is a well known tool frequently used by nurses to measure a patient's pain. It is also commonly used when asking for customer feedback. In relation to the latter it is generally perceived that '10 out of 10' is the only score acceptable - this is problem focused and not as useful. However solution focused scaling does not put us under such pressure as we use it in the context of measuring positive change and 'small wins'.

Scaling the Turbine

We utilise scaling, not to point out how far we have to go, but rather to look at how far we have come. Recognising what is already working and building confidence through 'small wins' leads to the hope of achieving more. Also as change is a constant we look at times when we were higher on the scale, and ask ourselves how did we manage that? What was different then?

Essentially scaling identifies key activities that can be used as small steps. Solution focused scaling questions allow you to measure and realise where you are currently in relation to making your authentic contribution towards your future perfect.

Sir Edmund Hillary, the first man to summit Mount Everest, described how he only concentrated on scaling the mountain one step at a time. If he was to look up and see all the barriers and the thousands of feet awaiting him to climb it would be soul destroying and also it would take him away from what actions he could be undertaking in the moment. This is how he conquered the world's tallest mountain.

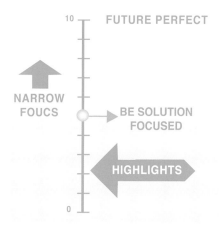

The goal of scaling is to:

- look at what you want,

- measure where you are currently as well as recognising what helped you get there

- identify what a positive next step might look like.

Now let's scale each blade with a solution focus. To enable this to happen I have outlined useful solution focused scaling questions.

Future Perfect Question

I have found that, as change happens constantly, people rarely rate themselves as starting at zero. However, it is okay if you do! You may find it useful to again revisit your future perfect on page 46 before answering this question.

1. Where are you now with regard to journeying towards your future perfect where 10 stands for the ideal state and 1 stands for the exact opposite? (Future Perfect)

Highlights Question

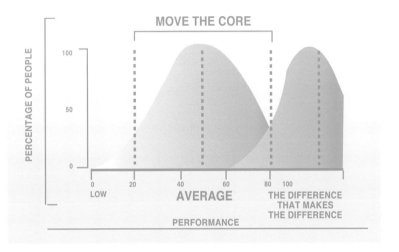

You will very often find small steps worth repeating amongst your highlights. By identifying key exceptions and strengths you can leverage off them. Focusing on your highlights especially in times of mass change will enable you to maintain a rhythm of what is working. They allow you to build towards your future perfect by learning from previous success stories.

Insoo Kim Berg (a solution focused pioneer) stated "there is nothing wrong with you that what is right cannot fix". So exploring what is "the difference that makes a difference" when things are going well will allow you to make the best of you the most of you. Now refer back to the Know Your Strengths tool on page 55 and absorb what stands out for you, before answering the following question.

2. How has your journey towards your future perfect managed to get to
   this point? What is the difference between 1 and where you are now?
   (Highlights)

Narrow the Focus Question

To keep up engagement and motivation it is useful to plan milestones
in the form of next steps on the scales - for example when marathon
running athletes often make promises to themselves such as: after the
next five miles I am going to give myself an energy bar.

The Pareto principle (also known as the 80-20 rule or the law of the
vital few) states that, for many events, roughly 80% of the effects come
from 20% of the causes. Pareto was an Italian philosopher who noticed
that 80% of Italy's land was owned by 20% of the population.

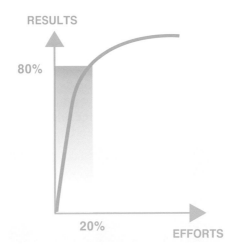

Examples

80% of effects come from 20% of causes

80% of your sales come from 20% of your clients

80% of health care resources are used by 20% of patients

80% of your complaints come from 20% of your customers

80% of the time we wear only 20% of our clothes

80% of crimes are committed by 20% of criminals

"If you want to go fast go slow."
Chinese Proverb

Let's utilise the Pareto principle within the context of making an authentic contribution. Focusing on the small steps you can make will help you progress towards your goal (i.e. future perfect) more efficiently. It takes a little discipline and focus.

You may find it useful to be mindful of the Pareto principle when trying to identify the small steps, i.e. the 80/20 key activities that will make the biggest difference. Remember the secret to 'the big' is 'the small' as it leads to positive change. You will now have a chance to list some small steps that will allow your authentic contribution to make continuous progress towards your future perfect by answering the following:

3. What do you need to get one step closer to 10? (Narrow the focus) What else?

As we have seen scaling enables you to have a clearer idea with regards to where you are in relation to journeying towards your future perfect. This enables you to see the small wins that have already been achieved, which creates more positive emotions and allows you to identify and amplify the highlights that will help you to continue. It also gives you an operational system to work from so as to keep up momentum.

FOCUS

5. Keep it Simple

Lastly and most importantly remember to keep it simple - you should be able to connect with it and instantly know how to work on activities that will make the biggest impact on your goals.

Summary of Part 2 of Chapter 6

→ Research shows that you should only select 2-3 goals at a time to be able to achieve them with excellence.

→ Goals which are not connected to your future perfect are less meaningful and more likely to end in failure.

→ Make your goals measureable by using the following simple formula: From x to y by when.

→ Keeping a compelling scale board motivates you to win.

→ When narrowing the focus remember Einstein's comment 'that everything should be made simple but no simpler'.

→ People like to overcomplicate projects they are involved in as it makes them feel superior and important however simplifying things is often more useful!

Your Authentic Contribution

7

Chapter outline

→ A Difference that Makes a Difference
→ What Teachers Make
→ Sample Authentic Contribution Statements
→ Your Authentic Contribution Tool
→ Share Your Contribution Statement

"Each of us has much more hidden inside us than we have had a chance to explore."

Muhammad Yunus

A Difference that Makes a Difference

The aim of this chapter is to incorporate and use the four components of the solution turbine so as to create your authentic contribution statement.

1. A solution focused mindset (Be Solution Focused)

2. Visualise a future perfect as your goal or your 'end in mind' (Future Perfect)

3. Leverage off your strengths and exceptions (Highlights)

4. Create a compelling scale board (Narrow the Focus)

Outlining the difference you want to make allows you to make the best of you, the most of you. It is about making the best contribution you can and in doing so being entirely yourself - AUTHENTICALLY. It is about accessing all that you already have to offer and moulding this into a meaningful plan. At the end of the day unless you are living authentically and with meaning, what are you doing?

What Teachers Make

The dinner guests were sitting around the table discussing life. One man, a CEO, decided to explain the problem with education. He argued:

"What's a kid going to learn from someone who decided his best option in life was to become a teacher?"

He reminded the other dinner guests that it's true what they say about teachers: "Those who can. . . do. Those who can't . . . teach."

To corroborate, he said to another guest: "You're a teacher, Susan," he said. "Be honest. What do you make?"

Susan, who had a reputation of honesty and frankness, replied, "You want to know what I make?

I make kids work harder than they ever thought they could. I can make a C+ feel like a Congressional Medal of Honor and an A- feel like a slap in the face if the student did not do his or her very best . . .

(Cont'd. . .)

83

be able to read your mind. All relationships are enhanced by communicating 'what matters most' to each party. Indeed in the same vein that organisations are not about 'communication' - they are 'communication'.

Share your contribution statement

"Whenever anyone goes to his or her associates and says, 'This is the contribution I plan to concentrate on and the results I should be expected to deliver,' the response is always, 'Why didn't you tell me earlier?"

Peter Drucker

To wrap up this chapter, doing what matters most is always something we are going to

get around to thinking about at some stage. So, be solution focused and passionate

about your future perfect now and the authentic contribution you plan to make to get

there. Find what you love and use it to serve others.

* An important point to note is that your future perfect and authentic contribution will be continuously changing and that is normal and useful. You can apply one for any problem or project you are involved in. In this chapter we applied one to the most important project that you should be continuously working on and that is YOU.

Summary of Chapter 7

→ Defining the difference you want to make brings a heightened sense of drive, meaning and purpose into everything you do.

→ Jim Collins stated 'it is impossible to have a great life unless it is a meaningful life'.

→ An authentic contribution statement engages you to consistently work on what matters most.

→ The authentic contribution tool enables you to craft your authentic contribution statement.

→ Like you an authentic contribution is forever evolving.

The Solution Turbine: Organisational & Team Success

8

Chapter outline

→ An Organisational Focus
  • Organistional Change
  • Strategy
  • Conflict Management
  • Performance Reviews
→ A Coaching Framework
→ High Performance Teams
→ Post Traumatic Success
→ Maintaining Propulsion

"Never doubt that a small group of thoughtful, committed citizens can change the world; indeed, it's the only thing that ever has."

Margaret Mead

This book has looked at how to use the solution turbine to make an authentic contribution predominantly from an individual focus. Below are brief outlines of how I apply the solution turbine more broadly within organisations and teams.

An Organisational Focus

The majority of people want to improve in the workplace and make a difference but frequently they are unsure how to do it. A recent Gallup poll stated that 49% of people did not know how what they were doing in their day-to-day job contributed to the overall goal of their organisation. People need to be able to view a compelling organisational scale board so that they know when they are making an authentic contribution and also so that it can be recognised and appreciated by others.

The solution turbine can be applied within an organisational context by identifying areas that are already working effectively and efficiently, called 'Islands of Excellence'. These 'Islands of Excellence' within your organisation can be examined

to ascertain the mindsets as well as the behaviours that the organisation's pivotal talent are involved in and which is having a positive impact on the organisation. By slowly moving the core of the people (i.e. the majority) to join these individuals, by modelling their behaviours, the business will see the areas of excellence grow. The more often you do this the more you start to recognise the desirable mindsets, behaviours and activities that make a difference.

Organisational Change

The solution focus is not a traditional expert led approach seeking to help managers dissect their organisation's problems and weaknesses, rather it looks at what is wanted instead. Pointing the solution turbine at the organisation amplifies what is required as well as instilling a sense of urgency to ensure its delivery. It is not an off-the shelf or 'one size fits all' approach as each organisation is different. A main tenet is to view organisations and their people as the experts on themselves. A solution focus approach involves asking useful questions, which is simple in essence but not so easy in practice. The solution turbine is there to assist organisations in realising their full potential - as Lewis E. Platt, former CEO of Hewlett-Packard, put it, 'If only HP knew what HP knows we would be three times more productive'.

A solution focused approach to working alongside an organisation would start by looking at what is needed to get right (be solution focused). What will be different when it is achieved? (future perfect). What will be different when it is achieved (future perfect). Identifying any exceptions or times when the sought after change is already taking place (highlights). Finally then outlining the small steps and key activities that the organisation can engage in to amplify the required change (narrow the focus).

Strategy

Most strategies fail when the majority of employees do not feel meaningfully involved and therefore engage little in its execution. A culture exists around what most people are doing most of the time and a solution focused approach to strategy is one which rallies most people to march proactively in the required direction. In brief it starts by looking at what is needed to get right in terms of success factors (be solution focused). It takes a leap into the future to illustrate what will be different once it is achieved and to look at what organisational success looks and feels like (future perfect). The creation of a compelling scale board so as to monitor the progress being made on the success factors deemed as necessary to reach the desired end in mind (narrow the focus).

Conflict Management

The solution focus is the direct route to developing win-win relationships. Most people view conflict within a problem view and cannot agree on what or who caused the problem. When focusing on what they can influence (be solution focused) individuals begin to close the gap in their thinking and positioning by narrating what they would like instead (future perfect) and when they have previously seen their relationship working better (highlights). This allows for the identification of possible next steps which could facilitate a win-win outcome (narrow the focus).

Performance Reviews

Most employees do not like either giving or receiving performance reviews. This leaves many organisations with a system which was designed to enhance performance actually slowing it down and damaging trust levels. Employees often perceive themselves to have been unfairly treated during a performance review process and are left feeling anything but motivated or inspired. A solution focused approach to performance is one which ignites performance by building solution talk within a performance discussion. The result being that performance improves and relationships are strengthened.

Solution focused performance conversations are based around what is within the team leader and team member's solution triangle, consisting of all that can be influenced and achieved (be solution focused). It is future and goal-oriented and the goals are agreed between the team leader and the team member (future perfect) as opposed to the main discussion being around the details of problems which have occurred during the period under review. The discussion is directed around what is working well and strengths that are being utilised (highlights) and around key activities that are predictive of success for both the individual and the organisation which encourages change (narrow the focus).

A Coaching Framework

The solution turbine can be used to coach yourself or others by asking the following solution focused questions.

1. Be Solution Focused
- What do you need to get right?

2. Future Perfect
- Suppose some time has passed and what you need to get right is happening, how would you know? What would you be doing differently?

3. Highlights
- What is already working in the right direction?

- When has the problem not being there or happening less?

- What strengths were you utilising at the time?

4. Narrow the Focus
- On a scale of 1 to 10, where 1 represents the problem at its worst and 10 your future perfect, where are you currently?

- How did you manage to get this far?

- How would you know that you have moved one step higher on the scale?

High Performance Teams

High performance teams are aware of the contribution that each team member is trying to make. Using the solution turbine is especially useful when a team is stuck, problem focused, experiencing low morale and trust levels. In this context it is possible to decipher which blade would be most useful to start with by looking at the questions below:

- Do we need to address predominantly problem focused mindsets and how we are 'viewing' to change the 'doing'? Is what we are doing not working?

  (Be Solution Focused)

- Are we unclear about our team purpose and what the team's most important goals are?

  (Future Perfect)

- Are we predominantly highlighting team member's lack of resources? Do we know what strengths exist in the team that will help us achieve our goals?

  (Highlights)

- Are we stuck, does change seem unlikely or difficult? Does everybody know the key activities to engage in that will be most impactful towards achieving the team's most important goals?

  (Narrow the Focus)

- Is creativity and innovation stifled? Are team members displaying a lack of initiative and confidence?

  (Positive Emotion)

Post Traumatic Success

Prevention is better than cure, for instance it is far easier to prevent a mental illness than to try to cure it once you have it. The solution turbine is best used when change appears hard and when you want to make an authentic contribution at an individual, team or organisational level.

Psychologist Martin Seligman was successfully awarded a Government tender in 2010 to provide resilience training to the U.S. army. Soldiers have often come home from the battlefield and suffered post traumatic stress which has left them unable to work in many cases. This was a major concern for the U.S. Government on two fronts firstly for the welfare of these young soldiers but also in terms of implications for the healthcare budget, as these soldiers can often need care for the rest of their lives. It is hoped that training the soldiers in positive psychology prior to going to war will be more beneficial than trying to fix them when they return home. Some soldiers (who have undertaken the training) are now reporting post traumatic success and are actually even more mentally resilient than they were prior to combat. Early assessment and feedback indicates that the initiative is working extremely well.

An example from the sporting world is Irish golfer Rory McIlroy, who won the US Open in 2011. He stated that if it wasn't for the mental 'speed wobble' he experienced two months previously during the Augusta Masters championship (which saw him let the Masters title slip from his grasp) he would not have gone on to win the US Open. McIlroy admitted that his Augusta meltdown inspired him to victory. So he not only bounced back from the set-back but actually capitalised on it and became even more steely and resilient.

"Problem talk creates problems; solution talk creates solutions."

Steve de Shazer

You can increase solution talk by flowing with the turbine and not against it. A problem focus tries to push against the wind of change and at the extreme people feel like they have being whiplashed, stunned, exhausted or overwhelmed into silence.

You can inspire solution focused thinking by making solution focused statements along whichever blade you believe would be most useful to you at a particular time. Here are some examples of how to do just that.

- It seems to me what helped us to respond effectively before was....(Be Solution Focused)

- So what we're saying is the next time we would like (x,y and z) to happen (Future Perfect)

- One of the things I thought went well last time was.... (Highlights)

- A sign of progress would be... (Narrow the Focus)

Furthermore if you need to do any of the following you can refer to the relevant blade for inspiration, ideas and useful questions!

- Clarity around what we need to get right (Be Solution Focused)

- To pay attention to what is

desired instead of the problem (Future Perfect).

- Explore times when (tiny parts of) the solution are already present (Highlights).

- Validation of all available resources and strengths (Highlights).

- To make changes towards what is better (Narrow the Focus).

- Enhanced creativity and critical thinking (Positive Emotion).

Negative emotional reactions act on you, as they act out of a survival instinct or wanting to preserve an interest. However to ensure you have more positive emotional reactions you need to act on them in the moment of choice. How best to do this is to consistently respond using the solution turbine, and thereby reap the benefits of the science of positive psychology and high performance to get better results time and time again.

This chapter explored a few ideas around maintaining propulsion so as to keep positive change happening. In essence the solution turbine is a model that allows you to utilise the power of positive psychology. It is most impactful when you need enhanced resilience and want to take a positive approach to change. The more you use it the more accessible it will be when you most need it. However it is not about putting yourself under immense pressure to be perfect or to have everything right all the time, as that would be a problem focused approach to using the model.

Summary of Chapter 8

→ By frequently propelling the solution turbine you ensure it will be accessible when you need it most.

→ Organisations traditionally focus on what's wrong or broken however the solution turbine enables them to identify what is already working well and enables them to amplify it around the entire business.

→ Regularly coach yourself with the solution turbine to ensure you are operating at your ideal performance state.

→ Teams that engage with the solution turbine continuously maximise their performance.

→ Only organisations that equip their people and enable them to take a positive approach to inevitable change will sustain and flourish.

→ Training yourself to use the solution turbine means you will experience rapid growth and enhanced resilience even when set backs arise.

→ The solution turbine provides a new mindset, skill-set and tool-set for:

- High Performance Individuals
- Managing Change
- Coaching Programmes
- Team Development
- Conflict Management
- Performance Management
- Strategic Planning

9 How I Got Here

Chapter outline

→ A brief history of the solution focus
→ Clues

"The reasonable man adapts himself to the world; the unreasonable one persists in trying to adapt the world to himself. Therefore, all progress depends on the unreasonable man. "

George Bernard Shaw

As a newly qualified psychologist I started my career full of hope and aspirations. Sadly, I soon became disillusioned as I realised my journey would consist mainly of analysis of those aspects of people's lives which were broken or failing. This in-depth analysis of depressed viewpoints was depressing in itself.

Originally psychologists believed that if we fully understood what made someone depressed or if we could understand a problem in its entire complexity then all aspects of a person's life should begin to function optimally. The focus was entirely on what was not working. Of course we can learn from mistakes but the opposite of failure is not necessarily success. Indeed we have much more chance of achieving success if we focus primarily on what it looks like to us individually, as well as looking at what is already working in our lives that can assist us towards it.

"Education is not the filling a bucket, but the lighting of a fire."

William Butler Yeats

It was not until the positive psychology movement grabbed my attention and imagination that I felt re-ignited. Positive psychology is a lot more than merely positive thinking or positive affirmations. It is a rigorous science that looks at measuring and anlaysing what in people's lives gives them feelings of hope, resilience, purpose and optimal well-being. In essence it studies what conditions make people flourish. Positive psychology was given a major boost from 1998 by psychologist Martin Seligman (considered the father of positive psychology). After becoming President of the American Psychological Association he used his tenure to give the field the credence and attention which he passionately believed it deserved.

This interest in positive psychology led me to solution focused therapy. The more I learnt about solution focused therapy the more passionate I became, as I discovered the potential that this therapy had to act as a vehicle to harness the power of positive psychology into people's lives.

"Solution focused therapy is simple but not easy."

Steve de Shazer

The solution focus approach started with a group of far out thinking therapists including Steve de Shazer and Insoo Kim Berg who set up the Brief Family Therapy Centre in Milwaukee during the early 1980s. They made serious breakthroughs with clients by asking them what they wanted to be better in their lives rather than spending all their time in therapy having conversations about their problems. They were reporting and seeing extraordinary results much more quickly than more traditional long term psychotherapies.

"The essence of long-term therapy is to create the illusion that you can make life not be one damn thing after another."

John Weakland

In the solution focused therapy world problems are viewed as challenges and indeed as goals. It is a client-centred approach which seeks to 'tap the shoulder' of the client rather than to force a solution onto them. It seeks to respect each case as unique and each individual as authentic. The following Steve de Shazer quote sums up the principles he developed as a premise for solution focused therapy. "If it ain't broke, don't fix it. Once you know what works, do more of it. If it's not working, do something different."

Matthew Selekman, a solution focused therapist, further highlighted the following solution focus assumptions which also act as the undercarriage of my approach in seeking to help people to succeed.

- Resistance is not a useful concept

- Cooperation is inevitable

- Change is inevitable

- Only small change is needed

- Most clients already posses the resources they need in order to change

- Problems are unsuccessful attempts at resolving difficulties

- One does not need to know much about the problem in order to solve it

- The client defines the goal of the treatment
- Reality is defined by the observer, and the solution focused professional participates in creating the reality of the system he or she is working on
- There are many ways of looking at a situation, all equally correct

I have found the solution focused approach to be a compelling way to start applying the science of positive psychology to daily life.

When I use it

- If change feels hard
- To dismantle complexity
- To increase resilience
- To enable innovative and creative thinking

Resources:

For more information on the origins and various applications see The Solution-Focused Brief Therapy Association www.sfbta.org/

For information on various solution focused applications in organisations see The Association for Solution Focused Consultants and Trainers www.asfct.com

Summary of Chapter 9

→ Asking clients what they wanted instead of their problem marked a step change in thinking in the world of therapy.

→ The benefits arising from being solution focused are simple to understand however it is not so easy to do.

→ The solution focus is free from being shackled to any particular theory. It is in many ways a theory of no theory.

→ Certain clues enlighten us as to whether a solution focus approach is being undertaken.

www.InsideiChange.com

- iChange Programmes
- iChange Coaching
- iChange Assessments
- iChange Community

info@insideichange.com

In Association with:

iChange Further Reading

A Sense of Urgency
- John P. Kotter, Harvard Business Press, 2008

Brief Coaching: A Solution Focused Approach
- Chris Iveson, Evan George, Harvey Ratner, Routledge, 2012

Flourish
- Martin Seligman, Nicholas Brealey, 2011

The EQ Edge
- Steven J. Stein & Howard E. Book, Jossey-Bass, 2011

The 8th Habit
- Stephen Covey, Free Press, 2004

The Solutions Focus
- Paul Z. Jackson & Mark McKergow, Nicholas Brealey, 2007

Positivity
- Barbara Fredrickson, Three Rivers Press, 2009

Go Put Your Strengths to Work
- Marcus Buckingham, Simon & Schuster, 2007

Switch
- Chip & Dan Heath, Random House Business Books, 2010

Further publications in 2014, 2015 and 2016.

- → Managing Reward
- → Managing Diversity
- → Negotiating Skills
- → Burnout
- → Coaching Skills
- → Life Balance
- → Conflict Resolution
- → Influencing Skills
- → Mediation Skills
- → Assertiveness and Self-Esteem
- → Personal Development
- → Innovation
- → Compliance
- → Strategy Development and Implementation
- → Leadership and Strategic Change
- → Strategic Marketing
- → Entrepreneurial Skills
- → Managing Attendance at Work
- → Employee Relations
- → Improving your Writing Skills
- → Organisation Development/ Training
- → Change Management
- → Organisation Design
- → Energy Management
- → International Marketing
- → Governance in Today's Corporate World

- → Customer Relationship Management
- → Building Commitment to Quality
- → Understanding Finance
- → PR Skills for Managers
- → Logistics and Supply Chain
- → Dealing with Difficult People
- → Effective Meetings
- → Communication Skills
- → Facilitation Skills
- → Managing Upwards
- → Giving and Receiving Feedback
- → Consumer Behaviour
- → Delegation and Empowerment
- → Basic Economics for Managers
- → Finance for non-Financial Executives
- → Business Forecasting
- → The Marketing of Services

ManagementBriefs.com
Essential Insights for Busy Managers

Our list of books already published includes:

→ Be Interview-Wise: **How to Prepare for and Manage Your Interviews**
Brian McIvor

→ HR for Line Managers: **Best Practice**
Frank Scott-Lennon & Conor Hannaway

→ Bullying & Harassment: **Values and Best Practice Responses**
Frank Scott-Lennon & Margaret Considine

→ Career Detection: **Finding and Managing Your Career**
Brian McIvor

→ Impactful Presentations: **Best Practice Skills**
Yvonne Farrell

→ Managing Projects: **A Practical Guide**
Dermot Duff & John Quilliam

→ Marketing Skills: **A Practical Guide**
Garry Hynes & Ronan Morris

→ Performance Management: **Developing People and Performance**
Frank Scott-Lennon & Fergus Barry

→ Proven Selling Skills: **For Winners**
Ronan McNamara

→ Redundancy: **A Development Opportunity for You!**
Frank Scott-Lennon, Fergus Barry & Brian McIvor

→ Safety Matters!: **A Guide to Health and Safety at Work**
Adrian Flynn & John Shaw of Phoenix Safety

→ Time Matters: **Making the Most of Your Day**
Julia Rowan

→ Emotional Intelligence (EQ): **A Leadership Imperative!**
Daire Coffey & Deirdre Murray

→ iChange: **Invest in Changing Yourself**
Alan Lyons

→ Managing with Impact: **Focusing on People and Performance**
Conor Hannaway

→ Discipline and Dismissal: **A Helpful Guide for Managers**
Dr. Mary Redmond & Frank Scott-Lennon

Notes:

Notes: